Dietmar Plath · Sigrid Andersen

FRONTIER
Airlines

Dietmar Plath · Sigrid Andersen

FRONTIER
Airlines

*O*hne die tolle Unterstützung von Chuck Cannon,
Denver International Airport, wäre dieses Buch
nicht möglich gewesen.

*T*he publication of this book would not have been possible
without the enthusiastic support by Chuck Cannon.

Inhalt Content

Die Geschichte Frontier Story	8
Impressionen Impressions	38
Das Streckennetz Network	86
Die Tiere The Animals	88
Frontier Express	90
Die Flugzeuge Aircraft	92

DIE GESCHICHTE

Grizwald und Konsorten
Grizwald & Co.

**Die Geschichte von Frontier Airlines
und seinen Tieren**

*The story behind Frontier Airlines
and its adopted animals*

Der Airbus A318 von Denver nach St. Francisco hat seine Reiseflughöhe erreicht. Durch den Bordlautsprecher heißt der Pilot die Passagiere willkommen:
„Heute fliegen wir mit Grizwald, dem Bären..."

Grizwald grüßt vom Seitenleitwerk des Frontier-Airbus. Das braune Zotteltier ist einer von 60 Werbe- und Sympathieträgern, mit denen Frontier Airlines seinen Firmenslogan illustriert: „a whole different animal" – „ein total anderes Tier..." Und damit zum Ausdruck bringt, dass Frontier Airlines eben eine etwas andere Airline ist.

Frontier Airlines ist eine Fluggesellschaft, die ihre Tickets zu vergleichsweise niedrigen Preisen verkauft, Vielfliegern das Meilensammeln attraktiv macht und sowohl Urlaubern wie Geschäftsreisenden eine Reihe von Sonderangeboten und Vergünstigungen bietet.

Na und? Das kennt man doch von Billigfliegern. Und dann stopfen sie ihre – günstig auf dem Gebrauchtmarkt erworbenen – Flugzeuge voll wie die Sardinenbüchsen, beschränken sich auf das Allernotwendigste beim Bordservice, lassen sich Drinks und Snacks bezahlen... Oder?

The Denver-to-San Francisco A318 has ascended to its cruising altitude. Through the loudspeakers, the pilot's voice welcomes the passengers on board:
"Today, we are flying with Grizwald the Bear ..."

Grizwald waves from the tail. The brown, cuddly bear on Frontier's Airbus is one of the airline's 60 advertising media and sympathy bearers. They emphasise Frontier Airlines' corporate slogan: "a whole different animal". They are to convey the idea that Frontier Airlines is a somewhat different carrier.

Frontier Airlines offers flights at relatively low fares. They encourage bonus mile collection for frequent flyers and put on a series of special offers and discounts for business travellers.

So what? This is ever so typical for low-cost carriers. Next, they overcrowd their cheaply acquired second-hand aircraft like tins of sardines. In-flight service is reduced to the very minimum. They charge for drinks and snacks – or do they?

Bargains not necessarily "cheap"
Frontier is one of those airlines doing things differently by offering full service at budget

Airbus A318
Grizwald –
Grizzlybär/Grizzly Bear

DIE GESCHICHTE

Was günstig ist, muss nicht billig sein

Frontier gehört zu denen, die es anders machen und auch bei Niedrigpreisen den vollen Service bieten. Die Gesellschaft betreibt modernstes Fluggerät – Durchschnittsalter zwei Jahre! Bei der Möblierung der Kabine wird auf Beinfreiheit und angemessenen Sitzabstand geachtet. Die Sitze sind komfortable 84 Zentimeter breit und mit Leder bezogen. Drinks und Snacks werden auch auf Kurzstrecken angeboten und sind ebenso gratis wie das freundliche Lächeln der Flugbegleiterin. Und ein vielseitiges Unterhaltungsprogramm mit Live-TV, Spielfilmen und Spielen gehört ebenfalls zu den Selbstverständlichkeiten an Bord des „whole different animal".

Passagiere wissen das zu schätzen, wie ein Blick ins online-Gästebuch der Airline zeigt. Nie hätte er gedacht, dass er im Zusammenhang mit Flugreisen jemals das Wort „enjoyable" (angenehm, erfreulich, unterhaltsam) verwenden würde, schreibt da beispielsweise ein erfreuter Vielflieger, der nach eigenem Bekunden noch nie etwas in ein Gästebuch schrieb, weil er noch nie Anlass hatte, eine Airline zu loben. Diesmal jedoch habe ihn der freundliche aufmerksame Service, die Bequemlichkeit an Bord und das Unterhaltungsprogramm gründlich überzeugt. Ein Feedback wie dieses ist keine Ausnahme.

„Die kleinen Dinge sind's, die den großen Unterschied machen..."

Und das freut den langjährigen Frontier-Chef Jeff S. Potter, der sich durch solche Rückmeldungen in seiner Geschäftsphilosophie bestätigt sieht. Er sei noch nie der Ansicht gewesen, dass eine Airline ihren Job erledigt hat, wenn sie Fluggäste von A nach B transportiert, sagt der 47-jährige Manager, der eine „typisch amerikanische" Karriere gemacht hat: Sein erster Job war Tellerwäscher bei einer Catering-Firma auf dem Flughafen. „Es sind die kleinen Dinge,

fares. They operate brand-new aircraft the average age of which is only two years. Particular attention is devoted to cabin fittings providing sufficient leg room between the rows of seats. The seats, upholstered in leather, come at a comfortable width of 33 inches. Complimentary drinks and snacks are even offered on short-haul flights along with a friendly smile from a flight attendant. It goes without saying that on board of a "whole different animal" amenities also include decent entertainment: Live-TV, feature films and games.

According to the airline's on-line guest book, passengers value such an idea of service. A satisfied frequent flyer who claimed he had never commented in such a guest book before since he had rarely anything positive to say about airlines referred to a flight as "enjoyable", a term he never expected to use in this context. He praised the friendly, attentive service as well as comfort on board. The entertainment programme was also convincing. Such feedback is not an exception with Frontier.

Gegen Langeweile über den Wolken bietet Frontier seinen Passagieren ein vielseitiges Unterhaltungsprogramm mit Live-TV – 24 Kanäle stehen zur Wahl – Spielfilmen und Spielen.

Frontier's remedy for boredom above the clouds: a diverse entertainment programme including 24-channel live TV, feature films and games.

Airbus A319
Maya – Jaguar

die den großen Unterschied machen", sagt er, „die Kleinigkeiten sind es doch, die uns auf Reisen auffallen – angenehm oder störend. Und wenn wir erreicht haben, dass diese positiven kleinen Dinge für unsere Gäste den Unterschied machen, weil sie zu ihrem Wohlbefinden beitragen, dann haben wir unser Ziel erreicht."

Frontiers Slogan „a whole different animal" ist also keineswegs nur als Hinweis auf die gefiederten, pelzigen oder geschuppten Tiere auf den Seitenleitwerken zu verstehen. Er ist durchaus auch wörtlich zu nehmen. Die Unternehmensphilosophie des Carriers steht auf vier Beinen, und die wiederum stehen für das Besondere dieser Airline, für die vier Grundprinzipien: Erschwingliche Preise, Flexibilität, Gastfreundschaft und Komfort.

Und dem Management scheint es gelungen zu sein, diese Prinzipien fest in der Belegschaft zu verankern. Unterstützt wird das durch eine starke Mitarbeiterbindung, denn – keine neue Erkenntnis, aber selten genug beherzigt – nur zufriedene Mitarbeiter können auch die Fluggäste zufrieden stellen. Wer bei der Airline anheuert, genießt eine Reihe von Vergünstigungen, von Freiflügen über Zuschüsse zu Arzt- und Zahnarztkosten bis zur Ausbildungsförderung.

Bei Frontier wird Mitarbeiterbindung aber auch dadurch erreicht, dass beispielsweise die Arbeitsplätze getauscht werden können. „Crossbreeding" heißt das und macht den Job gleich interessanter. Bei einer Belegschaft von rund 6000 Beschäftigten ist das gerade noch realisierbar.

„27 Spielfilm-Kanäle und Live-TV..."

Darüber hinaus sind die Frontier-Beschäftigten ganz einfach stolz auf ihre Company. Kevin Shaw zum Beispiel, der von Denver nach Hamburg entsandt war. In Hamburg-Finkenwerder, an der Elbe, überwachte er einige Jahre als Projektmanager die Endmontage der Frontier-Airbusse in Hamburg

"Small details make all the difference"

Frontier's long-term CEO Jeff S. Potter is rather pleased about such feedback. He is convinced it proves his business strategy right. In his opinion, an airline's responsibility is not limited to taking passengers from one place to another. Potter, aged 47, is at the end of a career ever so stereotypical for America: On his way from rags to riches he set off as a dishwasher for a catering business at the airport. Potter further states that the small details make all the difference and that such details are what travellers consider pleasant or disturbing on their journeys. Potter thinks Frontier can only meet their target by succeeding in having all the positive details make passengers feel comfortable.

The airline's slogan "a whole different animal" cannot be seen simply as a reference to all the feathery, furry or scaled animals on aircraft tails. On the contrary, it must be seen as a metaphor: the carrier's corporate philosophy rests on four "legs", each of them representing what is so special about Frontier. Its four principle characteristics: affordable, flexible, accommodating and comfortable.

Apparently, the airline's management succeeded in rooting these principles in employees' minds. This is achieved by strong staff retention. It is not a new finding that only satisfied employees provide satisfactory service to customers. However, this insight is hardly ever heeded. Whoever signs up with Frontier enjoys a series of benefits including free flights, subsidies for medical and dental treatment and educational grants.

Another way of facilitating staff retention is job rotation. Dubbed "cross breeding" – a term borrowed from the animal world -, this measure makes jobs much more interesting. This is just about practical with a total of 6,000 staff.

Other than that, Frontier employees are simply proud of "their" company. Just like

Vom Tellerwäscher zum Airline-Chef - Jeff Potter hat eine „typisch amerikanische" Karriere gemacht. Von allen Frontier-Tieren hat der langjährige CEO den Bären Grizwald am liebsten.

From rags to airline CEO: Jeff Potter pursued a 'typically American' career. From all the Frontier animals, the long-term CEO has chosen Grizwald-the-Bear to be his favourite.

Airbus A319
Perry – Hornlund/Puffin

FRONTIER STORY

bis zur Auslieferung. Auf die Annehmlichkeiten, die den Passagiere in den neuen Frontier-Airbussen geboten werden, ist er stolz, als hätte er sie selbst erfunden und umgesetzt: „Die Kabinen unserer Airbusse sind geräumiger als die unserer früheren Flugzeuge. Und viel leiser. Das mögen die Leute. Auch die Kabinencrew weiß das zu schätzen, denn es erleichtert ihren Job. Und wussten Sie, dass Frontier eine der ganz wenigen Airlines auf der Welt ist, die ihren Passagieren unterwegs 27 Spielfilm-Kanäle bieten? Und Live-TV an Bord?" Er strahlt, als hätte er all das eingebaut.

Großartiges Team mit Werte-Kodex

Und der Airline-Chef ist stolz auf das Frontier-Team. „Es ist eine großartige Mannschaft", schwärmt Jeff Potter in Denver. 1995 kam er zu Frontier, wechselte vorübergehend den Job und kehrte im Mai 2001 zurück, als Präsident und Chief Executive Officer. Im Herbst 2007 hat er sein Amt an Sean Menke übergeben, Frontiers langjährigen Chief Operation Officer, bleibt aber Mitglied des Aufsichtsrats.

Potter und seine Vorstandskollegen haben die Werte definiert, an denen das Unternehmen sich orientiert. Dieser Wertekatalog soll die über 6000 Individuen zu einem Ganzen verbinden:

Sicherheit, denn „Menschen sind unbezahlbar". *Respekt* getreu dem Motto „Ein Mitarbeiter ist ein Nachbar, ein Kunde ist ein Gast". *Vertrauen* nach der Devise „Wir sind so viel wert wie unser Wort". *Zusammenarbeit*, basierend auf der Erkenntnis „Wir sitzen alle im selben Boot". *Wert und Nutzen* ausgedrückt durch das Versprechen „Bei uns wird die Extra-Meile nicht berechnet" und *Passion* mit der Zusicherung „Unser Lächeln ist echt".

Auch in diesem Zusammenhang spielen die Tiere auf den Seitenleitwerken der Frontier-Flotte eine wichtige Rolle. Sie sind eben nicht einfach nur Dekoration. Obwohl sie das natürlich auch sind. Im Zusammenhang

Airbus A319
Ozzy – Killerwal/Orca

Kevin Shaw, who was dispatched to Hamburg from Denver as a project manager. He spent several years in Hamburg-Finkenwerder on the River Elbe supervising the final assembly of Frontier's Airbus order until delivery. He is proud of the amenities offered to passengers on Frontier's new Airbus fleet as if it were his personal idea and achievement.

24 feature channels of live TV

Shaw praised the cabins, which are more spacious in the new fleet than in the airline's former aircraft, and pointed out that a lower noise level is highly appreciated by passengers. Even cabin crew value this feature as it makes their jobs easier. He wondered if word had spread that Frontier was one of the few airlines around the globe offering passengers four feature film channels during the trip along with 24 channels of on-board live TV. While mentioning these peculiarities Shaw beamed all over his face as if he had installed everything personally.

Great team – great values

The airline's CEO in Denver was proud of Frontier's team, referring to staff as "an excellent crew". Jeff Potter went into raptures. He joined Frontier in 1995, temporarily changed jobs and returned in May 2001, taking the position as Frontier's CEO. In autumn 2007 he passed his job on to Sean Menke who had served as the company's Chief Operation Officer for many years. Potter will remain with the company as a member of the supervisory board.

Potter and his fellows on the board of directors have introduced a set of values as a guideline for the company. It is meant to unite more than 6,000 individuals to a "whole". This credo includes safety, respect, confidence and combined effort. To Frontier, it is important that people's lives are priceless; that colleagues are neighbours and customers are guests; that everybody is just as good as their word; and that they are

FRONTIER STORY

von links/left to right:
Airbus A319
Holly – Kanadareiher/Great Blue Heron
Airbus A319
Klondike & Snow – Eisbärenjunge/Polar Bear Cubs

mit der Unternehmenskultur symbolisieren sie, dass jedes etwas Einzigartiges ist, so wie jeder Mitarbeiter, jede Mitarbeiterin. Und alle zusammen repräsentieren sie die Stärke, die Wärme, die Freundlichkeit, eben all das, was „typisch für Frontier" ist.

FAA Diamond Certification Award – achtmal in Folge

Und diese Haltung wird belohnt. Es kommt oft vor, dass Frontier in Umfragen unter Urlaubsfliegern und Geschäftsreisenden zum besten Low-Cost-Carrier, zur beliebtesten Regional-Fluggesellschaft gewählt wird. Und mehr noch: Acht Jahre in Folge gewann die Airline den FAA Diamond Certification Award. Das ist die höchste Auszeichnung, die die amerikanische Zulassungsbehörde zu vergeben hat. Diesen Award kriegt eine Fluggesellschaft nur, wenn sie einen herausragenden Sicherheitsstandard vorweisen kann, weil sie exzellente Wartungs- und Inspektionsteams hat. Dazu müssen 25 Prozent der Wartungstechniker ein zertifiziertes Training absolvieren, zusätzlich zu den Schulungen, mit

all in the same boat. The list further includes both customer value and passion, suggesting the airline will not charge for an extra mile and promising a genuine smile.

Even in this context, Frontier's tail animals play an important role. Not only do they make our planes look prettier; they suggest that everybody is unique, just like every single member of staff. All the animals are a reminder of what is ever so typical for Frontier Airlines: strength, warmth and friendliness.

FAA Diamond Certification Award – eight times in succession

Such an attitude pays: in surveys, Frontier is frequently voted "favourite regional airline" as well as "best low-cost carrier" by business and holiday travellers. As if this were not enough, Frontier received the Federal Aviation Administartion's Diamond Certification Award eight times in succession. It is the highest award presented by the American airline regulation authority. To receive this award, an airline must prove meeting outstanding safety standards by

Airbus A318
Montana – Waipiti/Elk und/and
Airbus A318
Humphrey – Amerikanischer Bison/American Bison

DIE GESCHICHTE

denen sie sich ohnehin auf dem Laufenden halten. Bei Frontier hat die komplette Wartungsmannschaft dieses Sondertraining absolviert.

5. Juli 1994: Frontiers zweites Leben beginnt

Mit 180 Beschäftigten und zwei Flugzeugen vom Typ Boeing 737-200 startet Frontier sein Comeback in der amerikanischen Luftfahrt. Die ursprüngliche Luftfahrtgesellschaft gleichen Namens war über 40 Jahre lang Denvers „Heimat-Airline" gewesen. Mehr als 87 Millionen Passagiere hatte die erste Frontier durch die Vereinigten Staaten befördert und sich in all den Jahren einen ausgezeichneten Ruf erworben – wegen des exzellenten Service ebenso wie wegen des ausgezeichneten Sicherheitsstandards. Doch all das half in den Jahren der Deregulierung, die gerade die Zahl amerikanischer Fluggesellschaften dramatisch reduzierte, nicht vor dem wirtschaftlichen Aus. Den Konkurrenzkampf an zwei Fronten in Denver – gegen United und Continental Airlines – verlor Frontier Airlines. 1986 übernahm Continental den kleinen aber feinen Carrier.

Sieben Jahre später trafen sich Vorstandsmitglieder der ursprünglichen Frontier Airlines gemeinsam mit einigen Newcomern der Industrie, um der alten Frontier neuen Schub zu geben. Sie sahen gute Chancen darin, die Lücken zu füllen, die Denvers Hub-and-Spoke-System offen ließ. Continental schränkte gerade seine Operationen von Denver aus, und in Denver entstand der neue internationale Flughafen, der den Stapleton Airport ersetzte. Der Zeitpunkt zum Neustart war gekommen, und einige der früheren führenden Frontier-Manager standen zur Verfügung, mit Pioniergeist und vielen Jahren Erfahrung in der Luftfahrt im Aktenkoffer.

Mit Büffel und Widder an den Start

Am 5. Juli 1994 nahm Frontier Airlines den Flugbetrieb wieder auf. Vorläufig flog die

Gesellschaft mit ihren beiden Flugzeugen vier Ziele an und beförderte im ersten Monat des zweiten Lebens 5922 Passagiere. Die erste Boeing 737-200, die von Denver aus startete, zeigte auf einer Seite einen Büffel, auf der anderen einen Widder. Jeff Potter lacht: „Ja, wir haben damals auf jeder Seite ein anderes Tier präsentiert. Im Vorstand haben wir darüber viel gescherzt. Es hieß, die Leute sollten denken, dass wir mehr als zwei Flugzeuge haben. Aber so war es natürlich nicht."

Und so blieb es natürlich auch nicht lange. Denn die wiedergeborene Airline legte einen flotten Start hin und flog bald auf Erfolgskurs. Bereits nach einem halben Jahr betrieb Frontier eine Flotte aus fünf Flugzeugen und gab 330 Mitarbeitern Lohn und Brot. Der ein-millionste Frontier-Passagier ging am 21. März 1996 an Bord und wurde mit Konfetti und Fanfaren überrascht. Und als die Airline ihren fünften Geburtstag feierte, hatte sie knapp 5.8 Millionen Fluggäste an Bord genommen und 1 700 Mitarbeiter unter Vertrag.

Frontiers neue Flotte kommt aus Europa

1999 trifft das Management der US-amerikanischen Fluggesellschaft eine bedeutsame Entscheidung: Die Flotte soll umgestellt werden, von Boeing auf Airbus. Eine US-Airline entscheidet sich für Flugzeuge der europäischen Konkurrenz! 20 Flugzeuge vom Typ Boeing 737 sind zu diesem Zeitpunkt für Frontier Airlines unterwegs. Am 15. Oktober unterzeichnet das Management einen Vorvertrag über elf Airbus A319 und A318, am 4. November einen Leasing-Vertrag über 16 A318 und A319-Flugzeuge.

Der erste Airbus A319 wird am 6. Juni 2001 ausgeliefert. Frontier-Finanzchef Paul Tate reist an die Elbe, um den fliegenden Hamburger abzuholen, mit dem die Flottenerneuerung beginnt. Auf dem Seitenleitwerk prangt Grizwald, der Bär. Bei der feierlichen Übergabezeremonie in Hamburg-

employing excellent maintenance and inspection crews. To qualify, a minimum of 25 percent of an airline's aviation maintenance technicians must have completed additional certified training besides keeping up with technical development by attending regular training sessions. All Frontier maintenance staff have completed this special training.

5 July 1994: Frontier's reincarnation

Frontier Airlines was relaunched and again took to the skies of American aviation. The airline took off with 180 staff and two Boeing 737-200s. Frontier's predecessor, an airline going by the same name, used to be Denver's home carrier for 40 years. Former Frontier carried well over 87 million passengers across the United States. After all those years, it had established an enviable reputation for excellent service and outstanding safety standards. However, this did not rescue the airline from bankruptcy when the number of airlines in America was drastically reduced in the era of deregulation. Fighting at two fronts in Denver, Frontier failed to compete with both United and Continental. Frontier was finally taken over by Continental in 1986.

Airbus A319
Lucy –
Kanadagans/Canadian Goose

In den frühen Jahren war Frontier Airlines mit einer Flotte aus Boeing 737-200 unterwegs, und jeweils zwei Tiere teilten sich ein Seitenleitwerk.

In the past, Frontier ran a fleet of Boeing 737-200 aircraft with two animals on each tail.

Finkenwerder schenkt Paul Tate dem damaligen Programmchef Mario Heinen ein T-Shirt mit Grizwald-Konterfei auf der Brust. Der Airbus-Manager zögert nicht lange, entledigt sich seines Sakkos und streift das Grizzly-Shirt über. Fotografen und Fernsehteams halten fest, wie Amerikaner und Deutsche strahlen, wie locker die Stimmung ist.

Ausschlaggebend: Die sieben Inches mehr…

War die Stimmung in Denver auch so strahlend? „Naja, es gab schon so einige, die unsere Entscheidung nicht verstanden haben", formuliert Jeff Potter vorsichtig, „aber wir hatten gute Gründe dafür." Welche? „Bei den Airbus-Flugzeugen und der Boeing 737 gab es in Bezug auf Technik und Wirtschaftlichkeit keine wirklich großen Unterschiede. Beides sind hervorragende Produkte", räumt der Manager ein, „letztlich hat die um sieben Inches breitere und damit geräumigere Kabine den Ausschlag gegeben. Denn: Passagierkomfort war uns extrem wichtig. Wir wollten unseren Passa-

Seven years later, members of the board of directors of former Frontier convened with other newcomers in the trade to give an old airline a fresh start. The odds were seen in favour of an airline filling the gaps in Denver's "hub-and-spoke system". At the time, Continental cut back services in Denver to just a few flights while an international airport was built to replace Stapleton. Time has come for a relaunch. Several of the senior managers of former Frontier were available, all of them with pioneering spirits and several years' experience in aviation.

Buffalo and ram take off

Frontier took on flight operations on 5 July 1994. For the time being, the airline's two planes served four destinations, carrying as many as 5,922 passengers in the first month of Frontier's new life. The first Frontier B737-200 to take off from Denver sported a Buffalo on one side of the fuselage and a ram on the other. Jeff Potter confirmed this with a laugh. He said that at the time Frontier presented two different animals on either side of the aircraft. Potter further mentioned there had been a lot of joking amongst the board of directors. They said people were to think that Frontier owned more than two planes which was actually not the case.

Things changed soon. The re-born airline followed the path of success after a head start. Six months later, Frontier's fleet was extended to five aircraft. There were 330 employees on the airline's payroll. On 21 March 1996, Frontier boarded their one-millionth passenger with lots of confetti and fanfare. By the airline's fifth anniversary, it had carried 5.8 million passengers and contracted 1,700 staff.

Frontier's new European fleet

In 1999, the board of directors took a crucial decision: Frontier's fleet should be switched from Boeing to Airbus aircraft. It is remarkable to find an American airline

von links/left to right:
Airbus A319
Sarge – Weißkopfseeadler/Bald Eagle
Airbus A319
Maya – Jaguar
Airbus A319
Stretch – Silberreiher/Great Egret
Airbus A319
Bob – Delfin/Dolphin

Airbus A319
Woody – Brautente/Wood Duck

DIE GESCHICHTE

opting for aircraft manufactured by Boeing's European competitor. At the time, Frontier ran its services with 20 Boeing 737. On 15 October of the same year, the board of directors signed a Letter of Intent to purchase eleven A318 and A319 aircraft. This was followed by another Letter of Intent to lease 16 A318 and A319 aircraft on 4 November.

The first A319 was delivered on 6 June 2001. Frontier's Chief Financial Officer Paul Tate had travelled all the way to Hamburg to pick the Airbus up – which marks the beginning of the fleet switching process. Grizwald the Bear was prominently displayed on the aircraft's tail. When the Airbus was handed over in a ceremonial act in Hamburg, Paul Tate gave a T-shirt featuring Grizwald on its chest to Mario Heinen, who was then Head of the Single Aisle Programme with Airbus. Heinen did not hesitate to replace his jacket with the grizzly-bear T-shirt. At the event, photographers and TV crews documented German and American smiles and the relaxed atmosphere.

Airbus A319
Lobo – Wolf/Gray Wolf

gieren in einem kleinen Flugzeug so viel Platz wie möglich bieten."

Und das tut Frontier: 145 Passagiere passen in eine A319, aber der Carrier aus Denver legt seine Flugzeuge nur auf 132 Passagiere aus. Und statt 129 Fluggäste, die maximal in den kleinsten Airbus passen, befördert Frontier in seinen A318-Flugzeugen lediglich 114 Passagiere. Beide Airbus-Typen sind in Ein-Klassenfiguration unterwegs, klassenlos also.

Der Airbus selbst überzeugte seine Gegner

Aber wie war die Stimmung auf der Arbeitsebene? Kevin Shaw in Hamburg erinnert sich noch deutlich an die erste Zeit, in der die Airbus-Befürworter eine Menge Überzeugungsarbeit leisten mussten. „Im Grunde hat das Flugzeug selbst seine Gegner überzeugt", blickt er zurück, „wer es flog, liebte es, nur wer Airbus nicht kannte, war dagegen." Andreas Vita, der als Pilot eine Reihe von Überführungsflügen von Hamburg nach Denver gemacht hat und Piloten-Kollegen auf Airbus trainierte, nickt

Significant extra 7 inches

In Denver, the atmosphere was not as relaxed as it was in Hamburg. Jeff Potter said, politically correct, that there were quite a few who failed to understand the decision for which there were good reasons. Potter admitted that both technically and economically there had not been any substantial difference between Airbus and Boeing 737 aircraft and that both products were excellent. However, the fact that the cabin was 7 inches wider and thus more spacious tipped the scales in favour of Airbus since passenger comfort was of fundamental importance. Potter said the airline wanted to offer passengers as much space as possible on a small aircraft.

This is what Frontier actually does: an A319 can hold a maximum of 145 passengers while the Denver carrier only operates a 132-seat configuration. In A318 aircraft with a maximum capacity of 129, Frontier only takes

Airbus A319
Andy – Gabelbock/Pronghorn

bestätigend: „Piloten sind Kontrollfreaks, Airbus macht diesen Job leicht. Da muss man das Flugzeug doch mögen." Die Testflüge, die Vita absolvierte, seien samt und sonders ohne Beanstandungen über die Bühne gegangen, und auch die Kabinen-Crews seien von Anfang an pro Airbus gewesen. „In einer geräumigeren Kabine arbeitet es sich einfach besser."

Stephen Schmees, Fachberater für mechanische Wartung, erinnert sich an harte erste Monate mit viel Widerstand an der Basis. „Menschen mögen, was sie gewohnt sind, Umstellungen sind unbequem", erläutert er, und die Umstellung von Boeing auf Airbus sei gewaltig gewesen. Rund 200 Mechaniker waren zu schulen, in 20-er-Gruppen drückten sie die Schulbank. Airbus habe damals das Training sehr professionell unterstützt. „Das lief gut", lobt der Amerikaner.

Nur noch ein Tier pro Flugzeug

Und noch eine Umstellung war mit dem Einzug von Airbus in die Frontier-Flotte verbunden: Die Airline, die mit dem Slogan „The Spirit of the West" durch die Vereinigten Staaten gejettet war, veränderte jetzt ihr Erscheinungsbild. Es gab nur noch ein Tier pro Flugzeug. Auf dem weiß lackierten Rumpf prangte nun unter dem Namen „Frontier" das neue Leitmotiv der Airline „a whole different animal". Die „Abziehbilder" der Tiere werden in Denver produziert und in Hamburg von unten nach oben auf das Seitenleitwerk appliziert. Danach wird die Oberfläche des Seitenleitwerks mit Klarlack vor Beschädigungen und Korrosion geschützt.

Als Erster grüßte Grizwald, der Bär aus luftiger Höhe vom Seitenleitwerk aus seine wachsende Fangemeinde, zu der übrigens auch Airline-Chef Potter gehört. „Grizwald ist mein Lieblingstier", lässt er wissen, „dicht gefolgt von Jack, dem Kaninchen, aber es gibt viele gute Tiere." Stimmt: 60 an der Zahl.

on 114 passengers. Both Airbus types are fitted with a single-class layout.

Airbus A319
Hector – Seeotter/Sea Otter

Sceptics convinced by Airbus

How about the atmosphere around working conditions? Kevin Shaw clearly remembered the early times: Airbus supporters had to put great effort into persuasion. Shaw thought, in retrospect, that the aircraft itself finally convinced sceptics. He claimed that those who had flown on it simply loved it while everybody unfamiliar with the aircraft had objected. Pilot Andreas Vita ran several ferry flights from Hamburg to Denver. He had trained several fellow pilots on the aircraft and confirmed that pilots were surveillance

Airbus A319
Jo-Jo – Amerikanische Schwarzbären/Black Bear Cub

Jedes Frontier-Tier ist eine Type für sich

Grizwalds Kumpels sind ein Bison namens Humphrey, ein Kojote namens Carl oder Larry der Luchs. Und jedes Tier hat seine unverwechselbaren Eigenheiten. So reibt sich Grizwald mit Vorliebe seinen zottigen Bauch, hasst Wartezeiten auf der Startbahn und hat verständlicherweise wenig Verständnis für Leute, die sich Decken aus Bärenfell ins Zimmer legen. „Willst du das essen?" lautet eine seiner Standardfragen. Naja, und mit Gewichtsproblemen zu kämpfen hat er auch… Übrigens: Im wirklichen Leben bringt ein erwachsener Grizzly bis zu 650 Kilogramm auf die Waage. Und ist damit ein Leichtgewicht im Vergleich zu dem Flugzeug, das sein Bild durch die Luft transportiert – die A319 ist fast 120-mal schwerer.

Natürlich hat Frontier Airlines wie alle großen Unternehmen eine Abteilung für Öffentlichkeitsarbeit. Die eigentlichen Unternehmenssprecher sind aber die Tiere. In vielfach prämiierten Werbekampagnen sind sie es, die einem breiten Publikum die Charakteristika und Vorteile von Frontier nahe bringen. Die Werbespots in Funk und Fernsehen haben Kultcharakter. Wer es nicht glaubt, sollte www.frontierairlines.com

fanatics. This characteristic was supported by Airbus, a fact making the aircraft popular. All the test runs Vita had performed gave no reason for complaint. Even cabin crew supported Airbus, saying that their job was more pleasant in a more spacious cabin.

Stephen Schmees, a Technical Maintenance Consultant, recalled hard times during the first months facing opposition from the base. He pointed out that people like what they are accustomed to and that changes were always unpleasant. The Boeing-to-Airbus switch had been an enormous project, Schmees added. About 200 technicians had required additional training classes in groups of 20. Schmees praised the professional support provided by Airbus, saying that everything had gone smoothly.

Just one animal per plane

And another change came along when Airbus moved in: the airline once jetting across America as "The Spirit of the West" altered its appearance. The number of animals in the livery was reduced to one per plane, and the planes now displayed "Frontier" and the airline's new motto "a whole different animal" on the otherwise white fuselage. The transfers with the animals on them are

Airbus A318
Clover – Rehkitz/Fawn
und/and
Airbus A318
Sheldon – Meeresschildkröte/Sea Turtle

Airbus A319
Sherman – Seehund/Seal

FRONTIER STORY

Airbus A319
Bob – Delfin/Dolphin

Airbus A318
Charlie – Berglöwe/Cougar

anklicken und dann auf „fun staff" gehen. Aber Vorsicht: Bei dem Spiel „follow the penguins", bei dem der gewinnt, der die Pinguin-Gang möglichst lange auf der Eisscholle hält, besteht akute Suchtgefahr!

Tiere aus Colorado fliegen für Frontier...

Die Sache mit den Tieren hat sich Jim Adler ausgedacht, ein Kreativer in der Agentur „Genesis", mit der Frontier von Anfang an zusammenarbeitet. Gegenwärtig denkt er mit seinen Kollegen darüber nach, welches Tier den ersten Airbus A320 schmücken könnte. Die A320 wird im Frühjahr 2008 als drittes Modell der A320-Familie von Airbus in die Frontier-Flotte aufgenommen. „Da müssen wir uns etwas besonderes ausdenken", sagt Diane Willmann aus dem Marketing. Sie entscheidet mit ihrem Team darüber, welches Tier in die Gesellschaft der Unternehmenssprecher aufgenommen wird. Seit der ersten Stunde ist sie mit diesem Thema befasst und liebt es immer noch. „Es gibt keinen besseren Job auf der Welt", versichert die Managerin.

Und welche Tiere haben nun eine Chance, auf dem Seitenleitwerk eines Frontier-Flugzeugs porträtiert zu werden? Die mit dem Heimvorteil! Diane Willmann erklärt das: „Da wir eine Regional-Fluggesellschaft sind, mussten die Tiere aus Colorado kommen. Wir haben damals einen Wettbewerb ausgeschrieben, und Fotografen aus aller Welt haben ihre Tierfotos eingesandt." Büffel und Widder bekamen als Erste den Zuschlag. „Dieses Flugzeug nannten wir unseren College-Flieger", blickt die Marketing-Chefin zurück, „denn es gibt in Colo-

produced in Denver. In Hamburg these transfers are applied to the planes' tails from bottom to top. The tail surface is finished with clear varnish to avoid damage and corrosion.

The first animal to greet his fan club from the skies was Grizwald the Bear. The airline's CEO claims Grizwald was his favourite animal. The bear was followed up directly by Jack the Rabbit. But he admitted there are several cute animals, which is true: there are 60.

Frontier's individual beasts

Among Grizwald's mates are Humphrey the Bison, Carl the Coyote and Larry the Lynx. Each and every animal has its own unique characteristics. Grizwald enjoys rubbing his shaggy stomach, loathes waiting on the runway and has little sympathy for people having bearskins in their rooms. His favourite question is "You gonna eat that?" Actually, he is overweight. Besides, in real life a fully-grown grizzly weighs up to 1,500 pounds, making it look lightweight compared to the aircraft bearing its image: the A319's MTOW is 166,500 lb, which means it weighs up to 120 times as much as the bear.

Like all other large companies, Frontier Airlines run their own PR department. However, the actual representatives are Frontier's "spokesanimals". In an advertising campaign that received multiple awards it is the animals who convey Frontier's characteristics and advantages to a broad audience. TV and radio spots have achieved cult status. Whoever is not convinced should go to the "fun stuff" section on Frontier's website at www.frontierairlines.com to find out. Warning: the game "follow the penguins" is highly addictive!

Colorado animals fly Frontier

The animals were Jim Adler's idea. He is a creative with "Genesis", an advertising agency Frontier have always worked with. Currently, Adler and his colleagues are

rado zwei große Universitäten, deren Wappentiere Büffel und Widder sind."

Heimische Tiere auf den Flugzeugen einer Regional-Airline – das leuchtet ein. Aber was ist mit Flip, dem Delphin mit der Flaschennase? Oder mit Joe, Jim, Jay und Gary, den niedlichen Pinguinen? Die gibt's in Colorado doch allenfalls im Zoo, oder? Stimmt, sagt Willmann, aber diese Tiere leben an den Zielorten der Frontier-Routen. Als Frontier sein Streckennetz auf Mexiko ausdehnte, gab es eine große Kampagne in der Öffentlichkeit mit dem Slogan „Schick Flip nach Mexiko".

Giraffen oder Elefanten werde man auf Frontier-Flugzeugen nicht finden, stellt die Marketing-Frau in Aussicht. Frontier fliegt nun mal nicht nach Afrika. Aber wird es denn auch bei weiterem Flottenwachstum der Airline ausreichend Tiere geben? „Kein Problem", sagt Willmann, „schon jetzt haben wir mehrere Bären oder Widder, in unterschiedlicher Umgebung, in unterschiedlichen Jahreszeiten." Und ihr persönlicher Liebling? „Das Pferd! Es hat so viel Energie, so eine Lebendigkeit, ist so typisch für Colorado." Sally der Mustang habe einen besonderen Platz in ihrem Herzen.

In den Beliebtheits-Wettbewerben, bei denen Frontier gelegentlich die Bevölkerung nach dem Lieblingstier befragt, stehen Larry der Luchs, Grizwald der Bär, Jack, das Kaninchen und Flip der Delphin regelmäßig an der Spitze. Sie sind es denn auch, die im Fernsehen auftreten und Einblick in ihre persönlichen Eigenheiten, Vorlieben und Abneigungen geben.

Larry der Luchs mag Ordnung und Sauberkeit

So behauptet das Karnickel Jack, das es liebt, von Stadt zu Stadt zu hoppeln, es habe dem Osterhasen alles beigebracht, was dieser für seinen Job wissen muss. Larry der Luchs, weiß die Ehre zu schätzen, Frontiers „Sprechkatze" zu sein, hasst verlorenes Gepäck, Haarknäule und schmut-

reflecting on which animal will adorn Frontier's first A320. A320 aircraft will join Frontier's fleet in spring 2008 – as the third type from the A320 series. Diane Willmann, in charge of marketing, said they had to come up with something special. Diane Willmann and her team are to decide on which animal will become part of Frontier's "spokesanimal" club. Willmann has been in charge of the topic from the very beginning of the project and she is still happy about it. She swore there was no better job in this world.

So which animals actually stand a chance to find their portrait on any of the aircraft tails? It is those with a home advantage. Diane Willmann explained that Frontier prefers animals indigenous to Colorado since it is a regional carrier. Photographers from around the world had entered their animal photographs into the competition held at the time. A Buffalo and ram won the first round. The aircraft featuring these two animals was then referred to as the "college plane" since two major Colorado universities feature buffalo and ram as their heraldic beasts.

It appears plausible that a regional airline features indigenous animals on its planes. But how about bottle-nosed Flip-the-Dolphin? How about the cute penguins Joe, Jim and Gary? They can only be found in zoos in Colorado. Willmann said that was true, but explained they were indigenous at Frontier's destinations. When Frontier extended its network to Mexico there was a major public advertising campaign saying, "Send Flip to Mexico".

The marketing executive denied the prospect of giraffes and elephants making it onto Frontier aircraft since the airline does not serve Africa. Willmann said that running out of animals when further extending the fleet would not pose a problem because up to now there were already several bears or rams in front of different backgrounds and in different seasons. Willmann's favourite is the mustang because it is so energetic, lively and

Sie sucht die Tiere aus und findet, dass sie den tollsten Job der Welt hat: Diane Willmann. Ihr persönlicher Favorit ist „Sally", das Pferd. „Es hat so viel Energie."

She picks the animals and thinks she has the best job in the wold: Diane Willmann. Her personal favourite is Sally-the-Mustang. "She's got so much energy!"

Airbus A319
Pete – Pelikan/Pelican

DIE GESCHICHTE

zige Abfallkörbe. Flip der Delphin, schaut sich gern „Findet Nemo" an und ist ein überzeugter Mexiko-Fan. Naja, und dass der Fuchs Foxy die Trägerinnen von Fuchsfellmänteln nicht besonders sympathisch findet, dürfte jedem einleuchten. Ebenso nachvollziehbar, dass sich die Pinguine vor Halsentzündungen und Warmfronten fürchten.

Frontiers Tiere sind derzeit zu 61 Zielen in 32 Staaten der USA unterwegs. Sie absolvieren täglich 280 Starts und Landungen. Knapp 90 Millionen Passagiere sind seit der Neugründung der Airline bei Frontier an Bord gegangen. Das Streckennetz der Airline geht quer durch die USA – von San Francisco im äußersten Westen bis Fort Lauderdale oder New York an der Ostküste, von Houston im Süden bis Anchorage im Norden. Im Flugplan stehen auch acht Flughäfen in Mexiko – Cabo San Lucas, Mazatlán, Puerto Vallarta, Guadalajara, Ixtapa, Acapulco, Cancún und Cozumel sowie zwei in Kanada – Calgary und Vancouver. Seit Herbst 2007 wird auch San José in Costa Rica angeflogen. 60 Airbus-Flugzeuge – elf A318 und 49 A319 sind auf diesen Routen unterwegs. 2008 kommt die größere

ever so typical for Colorado. She has a soft spot for Sally the Mustang.

Frontier runs surveys amongst the public asking for people's favourite animals. Larry the Lynx, Grizwald the Bear, Jack the Rabbit and Flip the Dolphin usually are in the lead. It is these animals who then appear on TV and let people have a closer look at their characteristics, preferences and aversions.

Larry the Lynx loves tidiness

Jack-the-Rabbit claims he loved hopping from city to city and having taught the Easter bunny everything it needed for its job. Larry the Lynx appreciates being the airline's "spokescat" while he hates lost luggage, hairballs and dirty litter boxes. Flip the Dolphin enjoys watching "Finding Nemo" while being a great fan of Mexico. It seems obvious that Foxy the Fox has a great dislike for women wearing foxtail coats. It is also plausible that the penguin band fear laryngitis and warm fronts.

Frontier's pets are currently travelling to 61 destination and fly to 32 US States. They complete 280 take-offs and landings every day. Just about 90 million passengers boarded Frontier planes ever since the airline was re-established. Frontier's network extends all across the United States: from San Francisco in the far West to Fort Lauderdale or New York on the East Coast; from southern Houston to northern Anchorage. The flight schedule also includes eight airports in Mexico (Cabo San Lucas, Mazatlán, Puerto Vallarta, Guadalajara, Ixtapa, Acapulco, Cancún and Cozumel) as well as two Canadian destinations (Calgary and Vancouver). In autumn 2007, San José in Costa Rica joined Frontier's network. All the routes are served by a total of 60 aircraft: eleven A318 and 49 A319. In 2008, the A320, the largest model in the A320 series, will join the fleet. The first out of the ten aircraft ordered is scheduled for delivery in spring 2008. The "alpha" animal to be on the tail has not yet been decided upon.

Airbus A318
Grizzlybär/Grizzly Bear

Airbus A319
O'Malley – Stockente/Mallard

DIE GESCHICHTE

Schwester der beiden kleinsten Airbus-Typen zur Verstärkung: Zehn Flugzeuge A320 hat Frontier Airlines bestellt. Die erste Maschine soll im Frühjahr 2008 ausgeliefert werden. Über das Leit(werk)tier wird noch nachgedacht.

Wind von vorn – auf einem stürmischen Markt

Derweil bläst dem Carrier aus Colorado nicht nur der Westwind aus den Rocky Mountains frontal gegen die Flugzeugnase. In jüngster Zeit hat Frontier Airlines zunehmend auch mit dem eisigen Wind eines beinharten Marktes zu kämpfen. Da ist zum einen die in Dallas ansässige Southwest Airlines. Sie rückte der tierischen Fluggesellschaft gehörig auf den Pelz, als sie 2006 Denver in ihr Streckennetz aufnahm und damit sogar einen Sinkflug der Frontier-Aktie auslöste. Der zweite starke Konkurrent ist Marktführer United Airlines:

Head wind on a dynamic market

However, the carrier is not only facing strong westerly winds from the Rocky Mountains blowing at its aircrafts' noses. Currently, Frontier Airlines have to deal with a strong, icy wind from a dog-eat-dog market. One of the strong competitors is Dallas-based Southwest Airlines, which challenged Frontier by adding Denver to its network, thus causing Frontier shares to descend. The other competitor at Denver International Airport would be United Airlines. The fire of turbulent competition is only painfully fuelled by a continually increasing fuel price that cannot be expected to "descend".

Sean Menke, the new dog in Frontier's management office, had to loosen several knots when moving in. One of the issues was the delayed establishment of Frontier's subsidiary Lynx Aviation. The first out of ten Q400 aircraft ordered from Bombardier was scheduled for take-off from Denver for

Airbus A319
Jack – Schneeschuhhase/Snowshoe Hare

Airbus A319
Flip – Großer Tümmler/Bottlenosed Dolphin

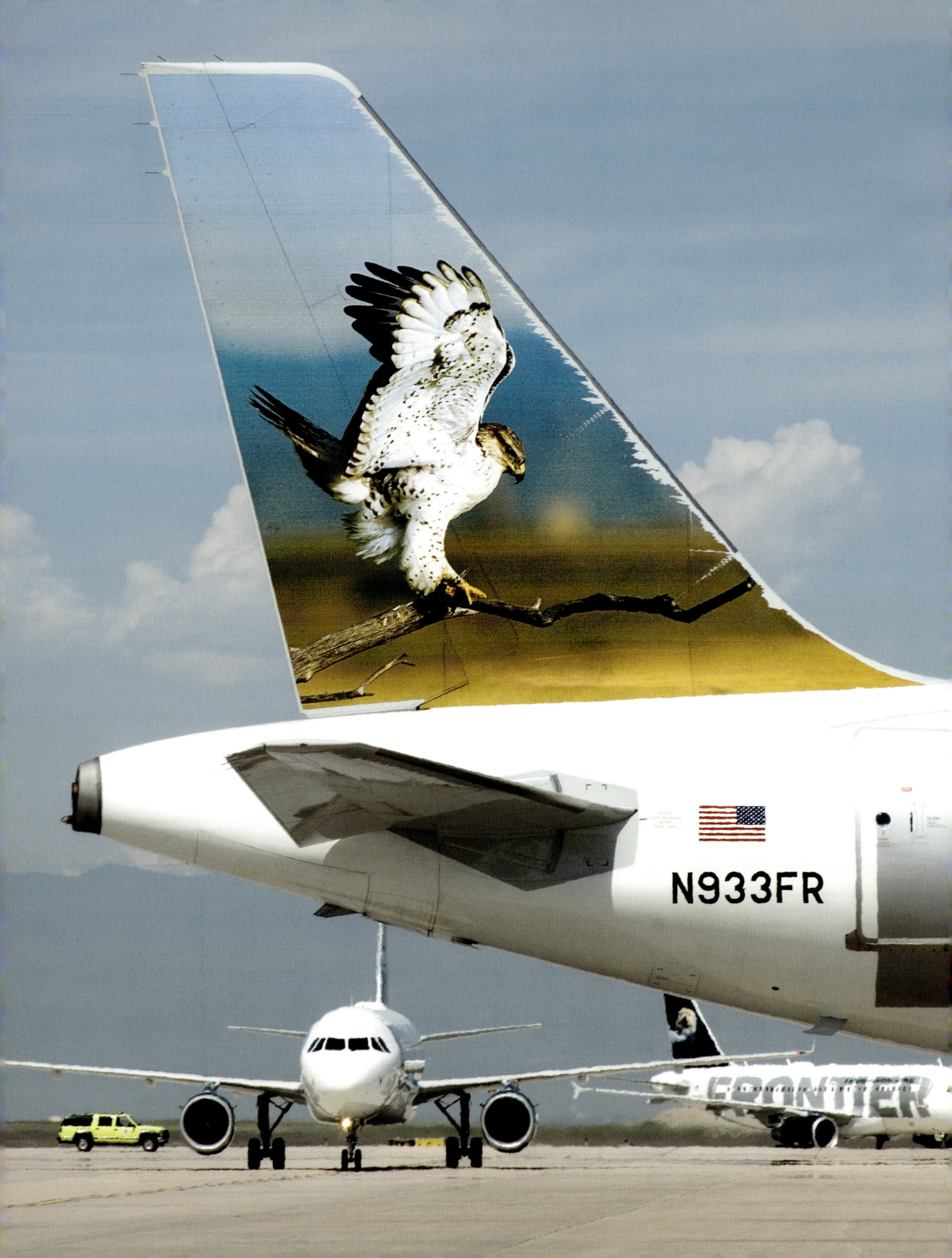
N933FR
FRONTIER

Auch United-Flugzeuge starten und landen auf dem Internationalen Flughafen Denver. In solchen Zeiten tun natürlich auch die anhaltend hohen Treibstoffpreise besonders weh. Zumal hier ein Sinkflug nicht zu erwarten ist.

So hat Sean Menke, der neue Mann im Frontier-Chefbüro, bei seinem Einzug allerhand Knoten zu lösen. Dazu gehört auch die verspätete Geburt der Frontier-Tochter Lynx Aviation. Das erste von zehn bestellten Bombardier Q400-Flugzeugen – das mit dem Luchs-Baby Larry auf dem Leitwerk – sollte ursprünglich ab Oktober 2007 von Denver nach Wichita abheben, und es war vorgesehen, in der Wintersaison mit der wachsenden Bombardier-Flotte in die Skigebiete der Rocky Mountains zu jetten. Der Zeitplan verschob sich, weil die Behördenzulassung auf sich warten ließ.

Kompetenter Steuermann – treue Fangemeinde

Um Frontier sicher durch die Turbulenzen zu steuern, bringt der 38-jährige CEO über 15 Jahre Erfahrung im Airline-Geschäft mit, darunter sechs Jahre bei Frontier Airlines. In den Jahren, bevor er in die Frontier-Zentrale in der Tower Road in Denver zurückkehrte, war er bei Air Canada für alle kommerziellen Themen verantwortlich – vom Marketing über Verkauf, Flugpläne, Werbung, Forschung und Produktentwicklung ebenso wie für internationale Angelegenheiten, Allianzen und den Charterservice Jetz.

Und es gibt einen weiteren guten Grund für die „total andere Airline", zuversichtlich in die Zukunft zu blicken: Die treue Fangemeinde, die den fliegenden Frontier-Zoo fest ins Herz geschlossen hat. Das drückt sich durchaus auch in Zahlen aus: Allein im August 2007 gingen über eine Million Passagiere an Bord eines Frontier-Airlines-Flugzeugs. Das sind 21 Prozent mehr als im August des Vorjahres. Grund zum Optimismus für Grizwald und Konsorten!

Wichita in October 2007. Frontier's agenda also extended to running the growing Bombardier fleet to skiing resorts in the winter season. However, it had to be postponed over delayed registration procedures.

Competent navigator – loyal fans

The CEO, aged 38, has some 15 years' experience in airline business, including six years with Frontier. This experience will help navigate Frontier through any turbulence. In the years before moving into Frontier's headquarters in Denver's Tower Road, Menke was in charge of business-related topics with Air Canada, ranging from marketing to sales, to flight scheduling, advertising and product development. His responsibilities also included international affairs, alliance matters and Jetz charter service.

There is yet another reason for this wholly different airline to be confident in excellent prospects. There is a loyal fan club with a soft spot for Frontier's flying zoo. This is supported by statistics: in August 2007 alone, half a million passengers boarded Frontier aircraft. This means an increase of 21 percent compared to the same month in the previous year. What a good reason for optimism for Grizwald & Co.!

Sean Menke ist ein Wieder-Einsteiger. Nach sechs Jahren im Vorstand „dieser unglaublichen Airline" wechselte er zu Air Canada und machte dort viele nützliche Erfahrungen. Die brachte er als neuer CEO im Herbst 2007 ins Frontier-Chefbüro mit.

Sean Menke is a returner. After six years with "this amazing airline", he switched to Air Canada where he gained great and useful experience. As the airline's new CEO, Menke brought this experience to Frontier's executive office in autumn 2007.

Airbus A319
Sebastian – Königsbussard/ Ferruginous Hawk

e Ht.

42 F

A whole different animal.

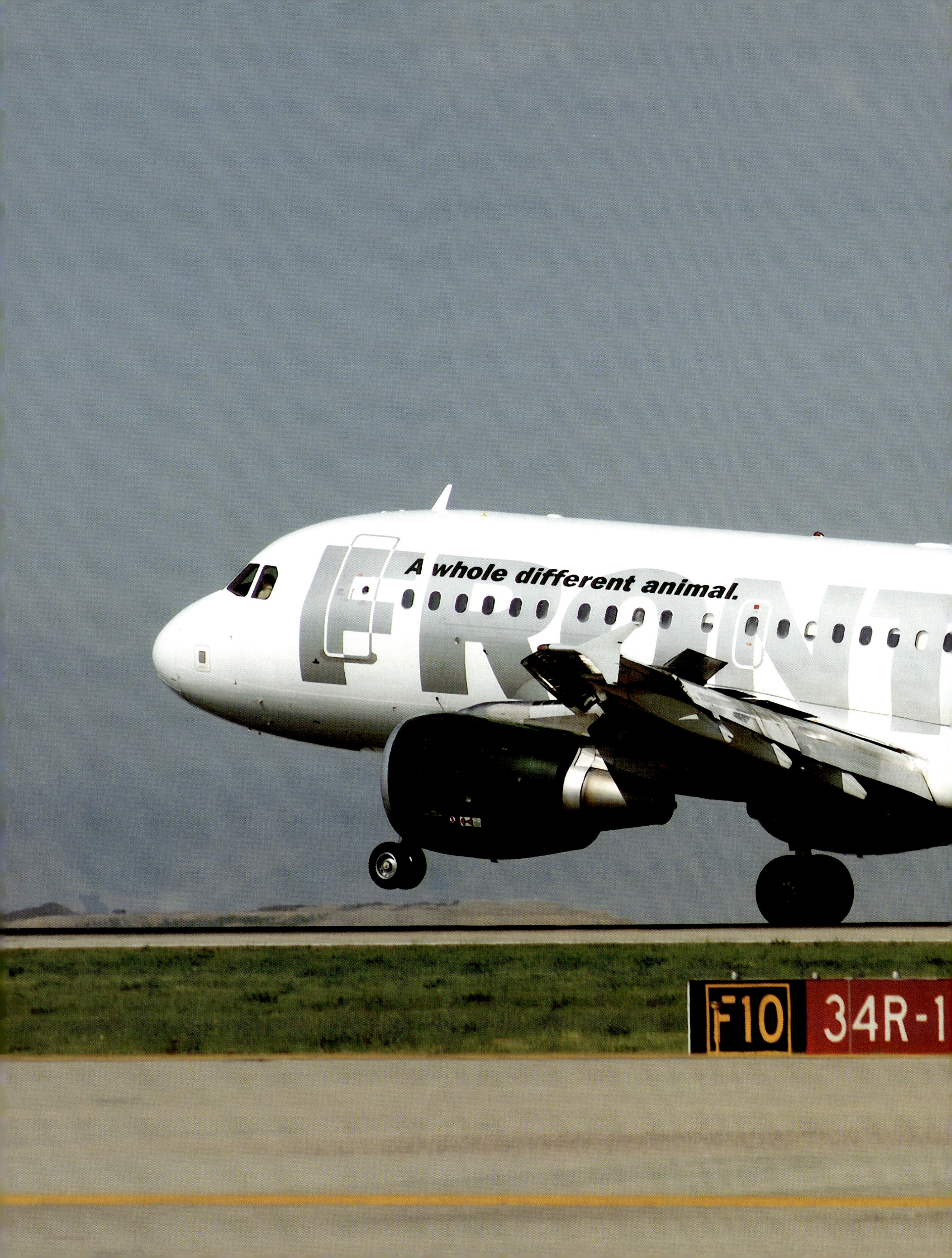
A whole different animal.
F10
34R-1

N804FR

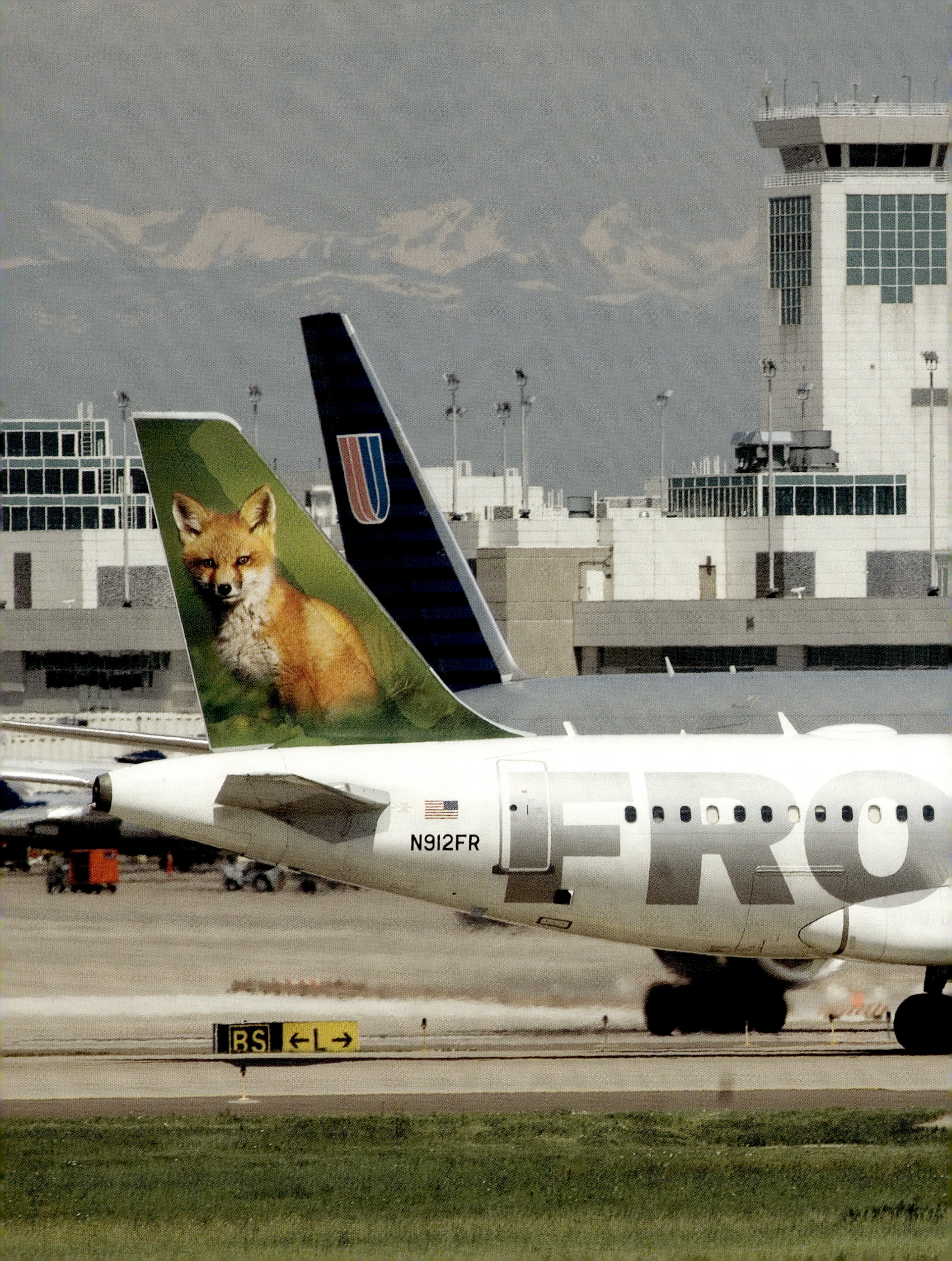
N912FR
FRO
BS ←L→

A whole different animal.

FRONTIER
A whole different animal.
N908FR
N922FR
N921FR
FRON
A whole diff

FRONTIER
A whole different animal.
A32
A34
N918FR
A whole different animal.
A36
A whole different animal.
A whole different animal.
A38
A26
A28
A30
FRONTIER
FRONTIER

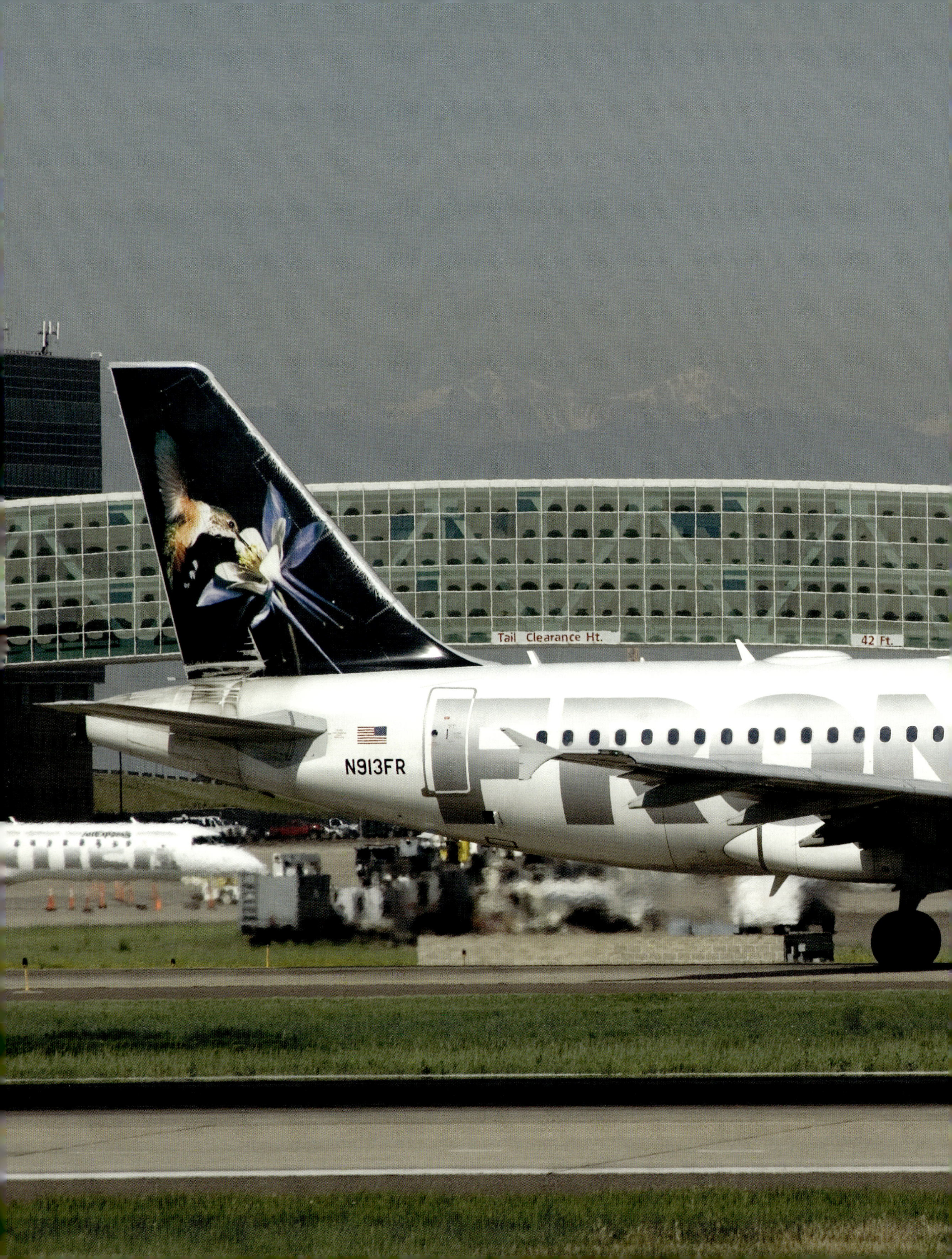
Tail Clearance Ht.
42 Ft.
N913FR

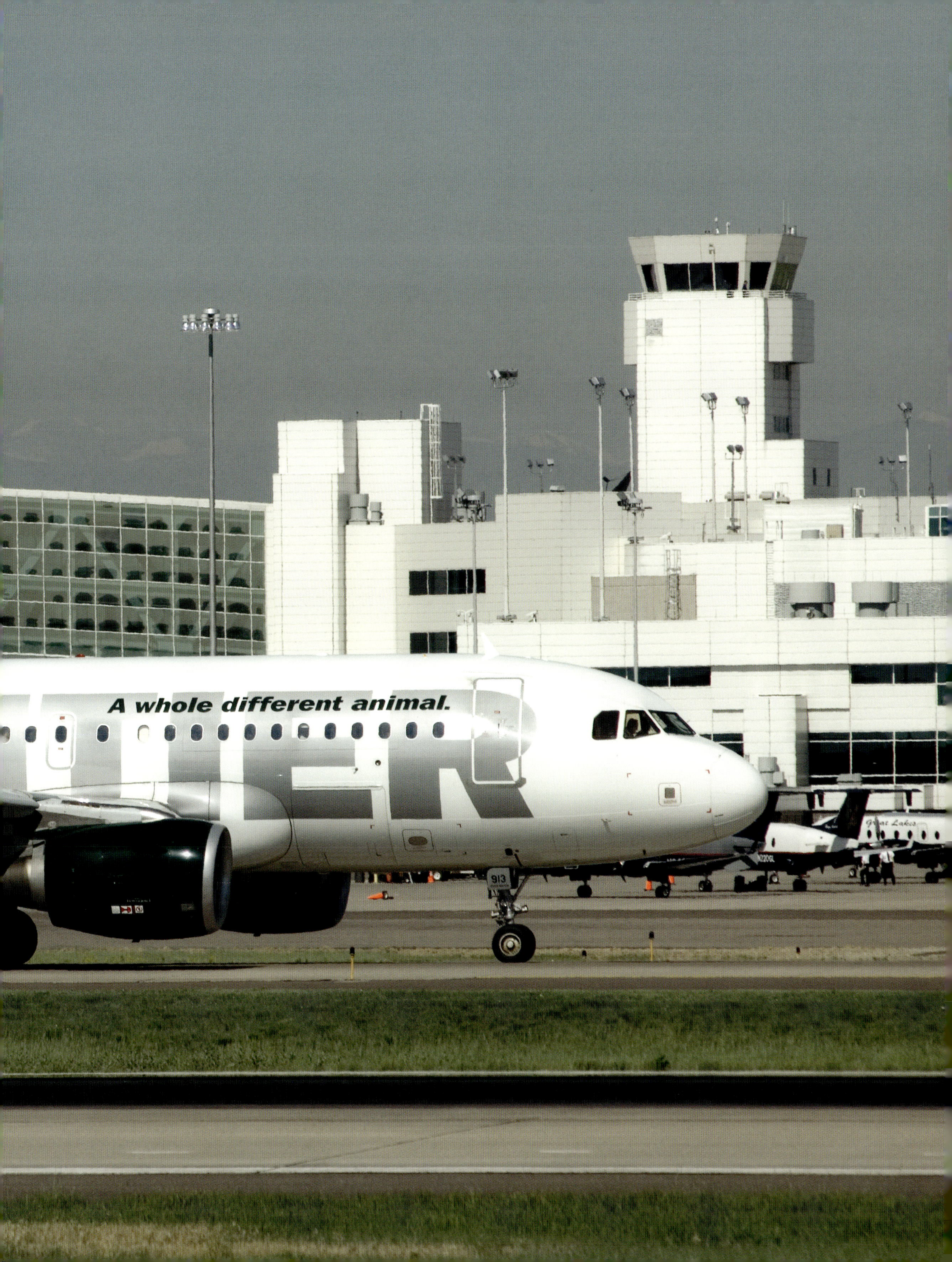
A whole different animal.

A whole different animal.

F4 34R-16L

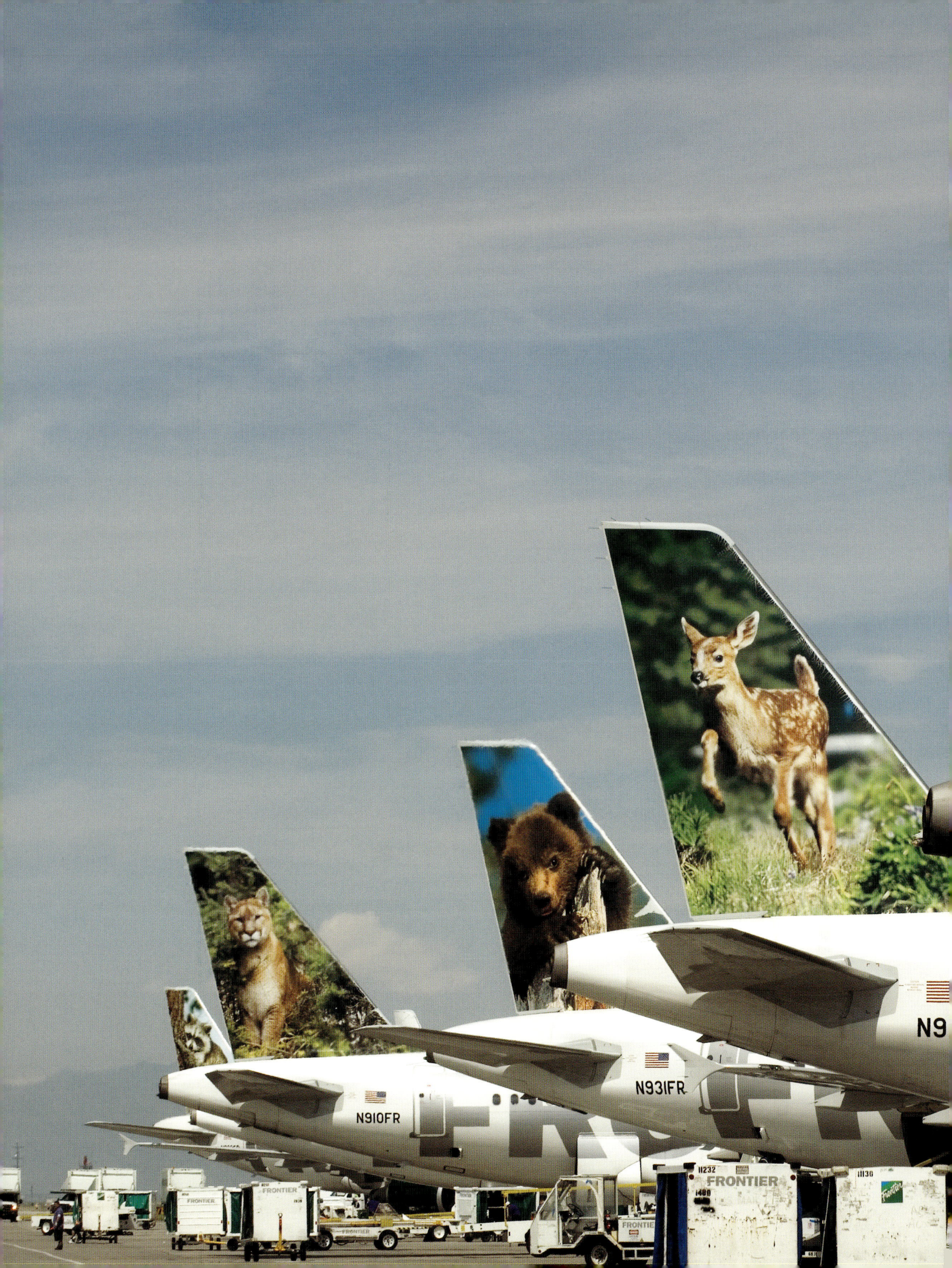
N910FR
N931FR
FRONTIER

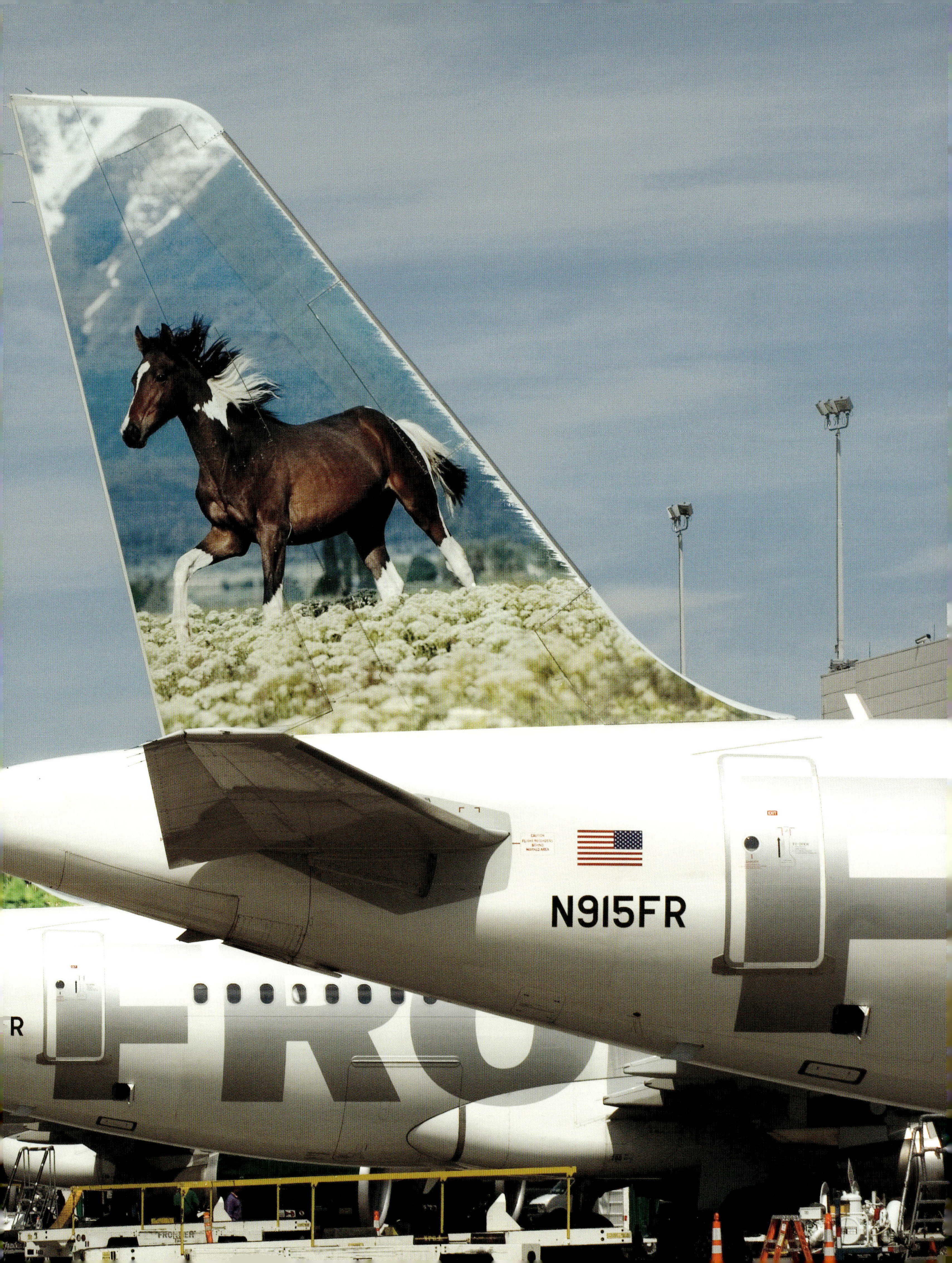
N915FR
FRO

A whole different animal.

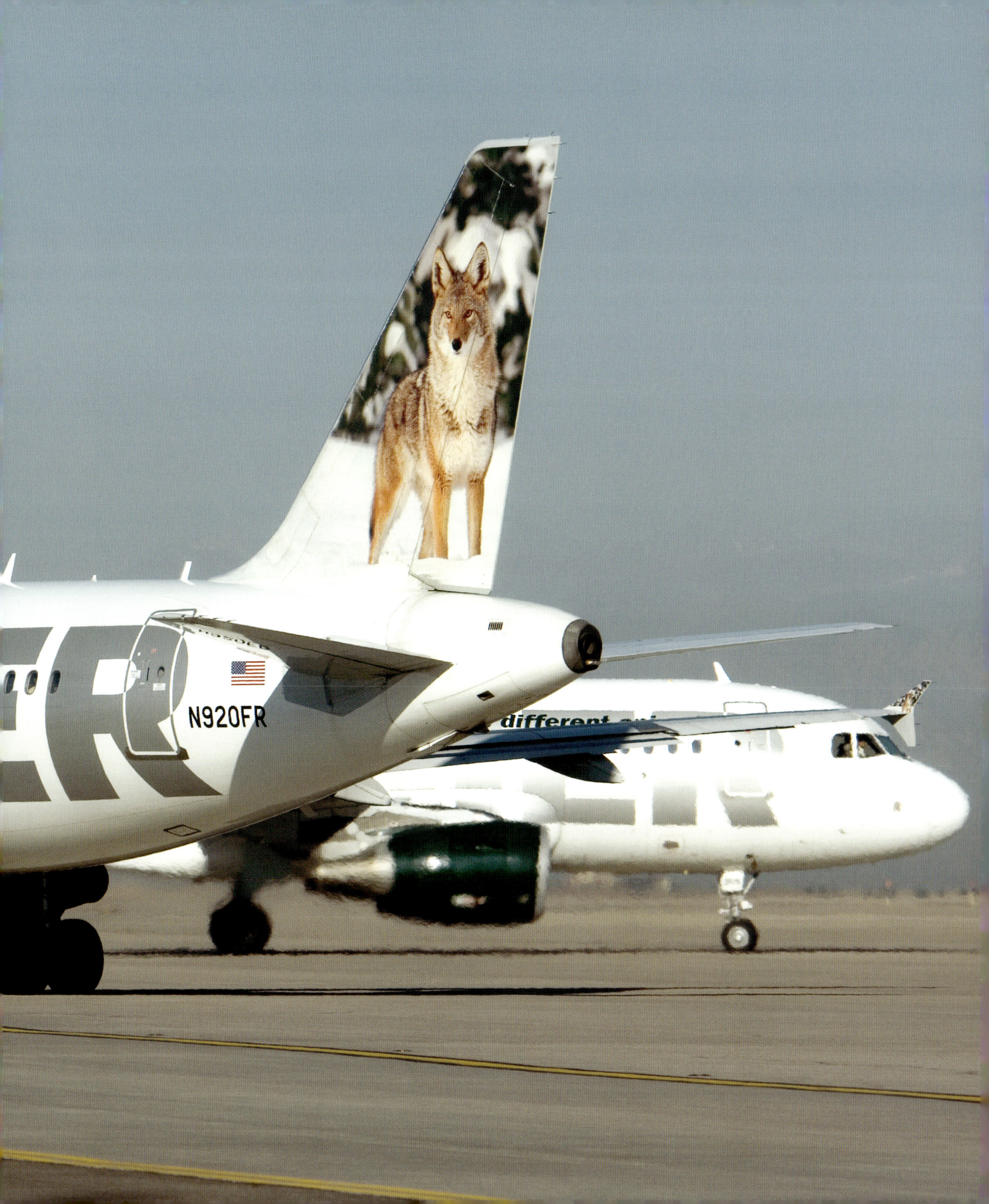
N920FR

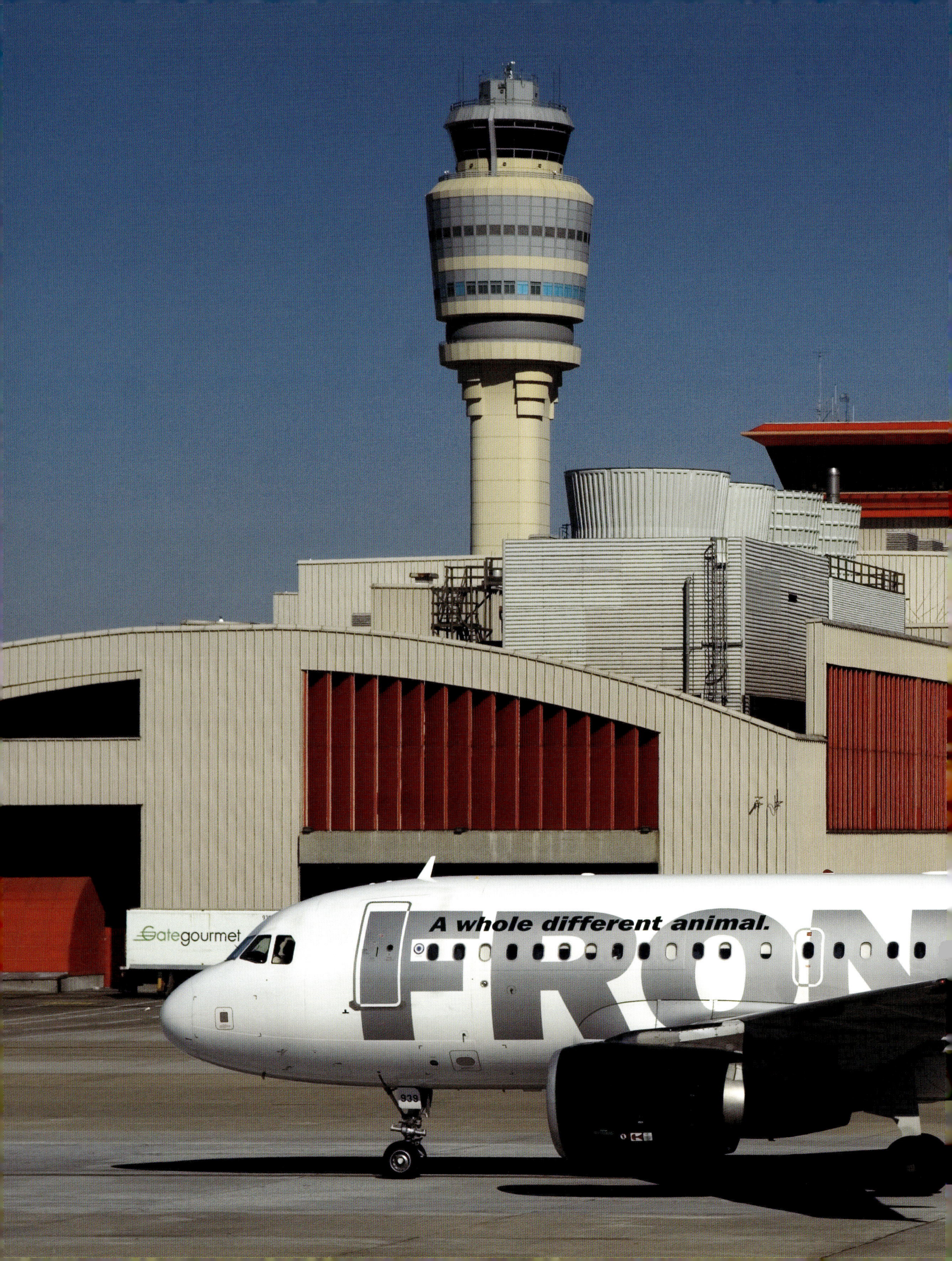
Gategourmet
A whole different animal.
FRON
939

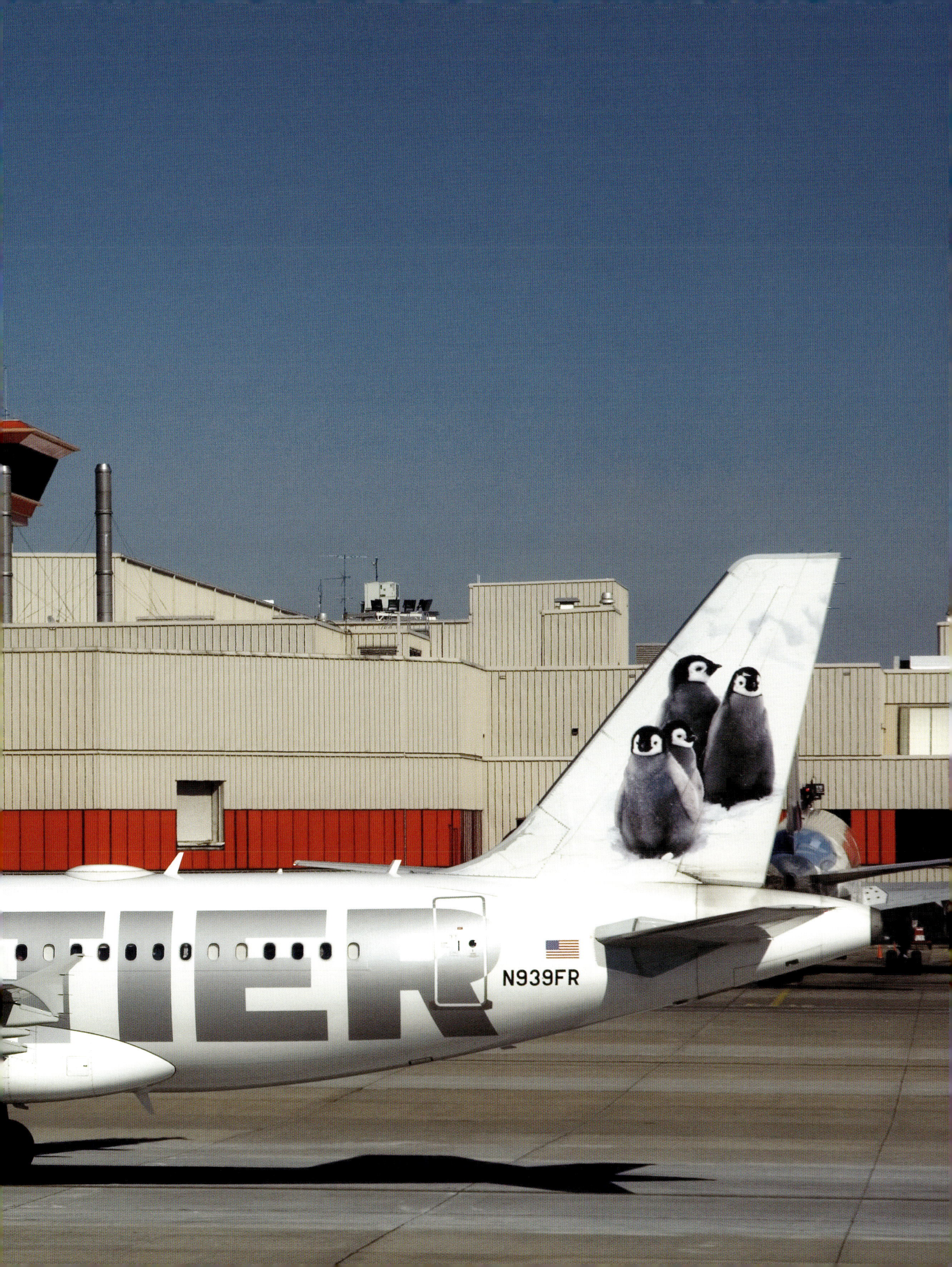
TIER
N939FR

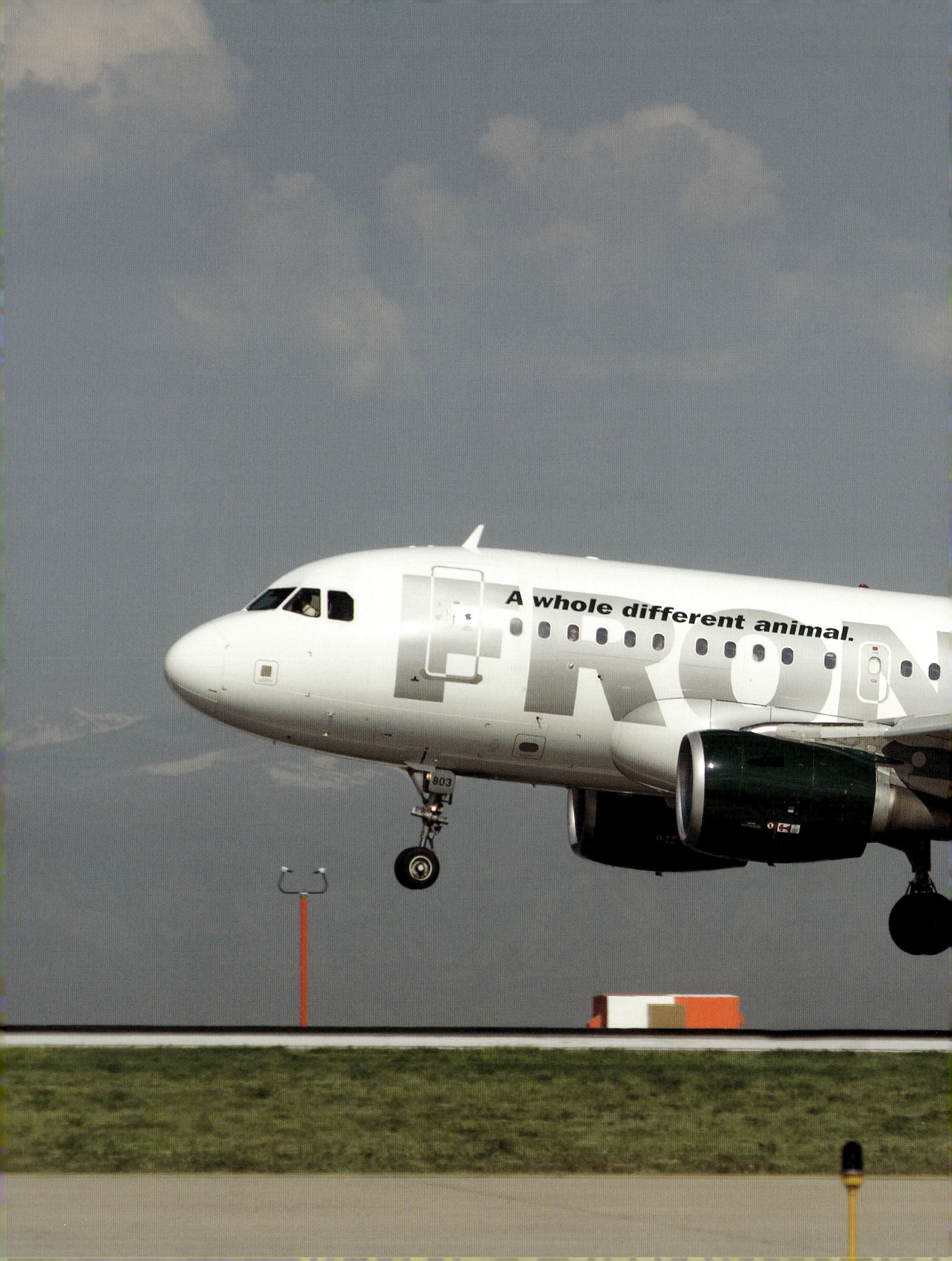
A whole different animal.
FRON
803

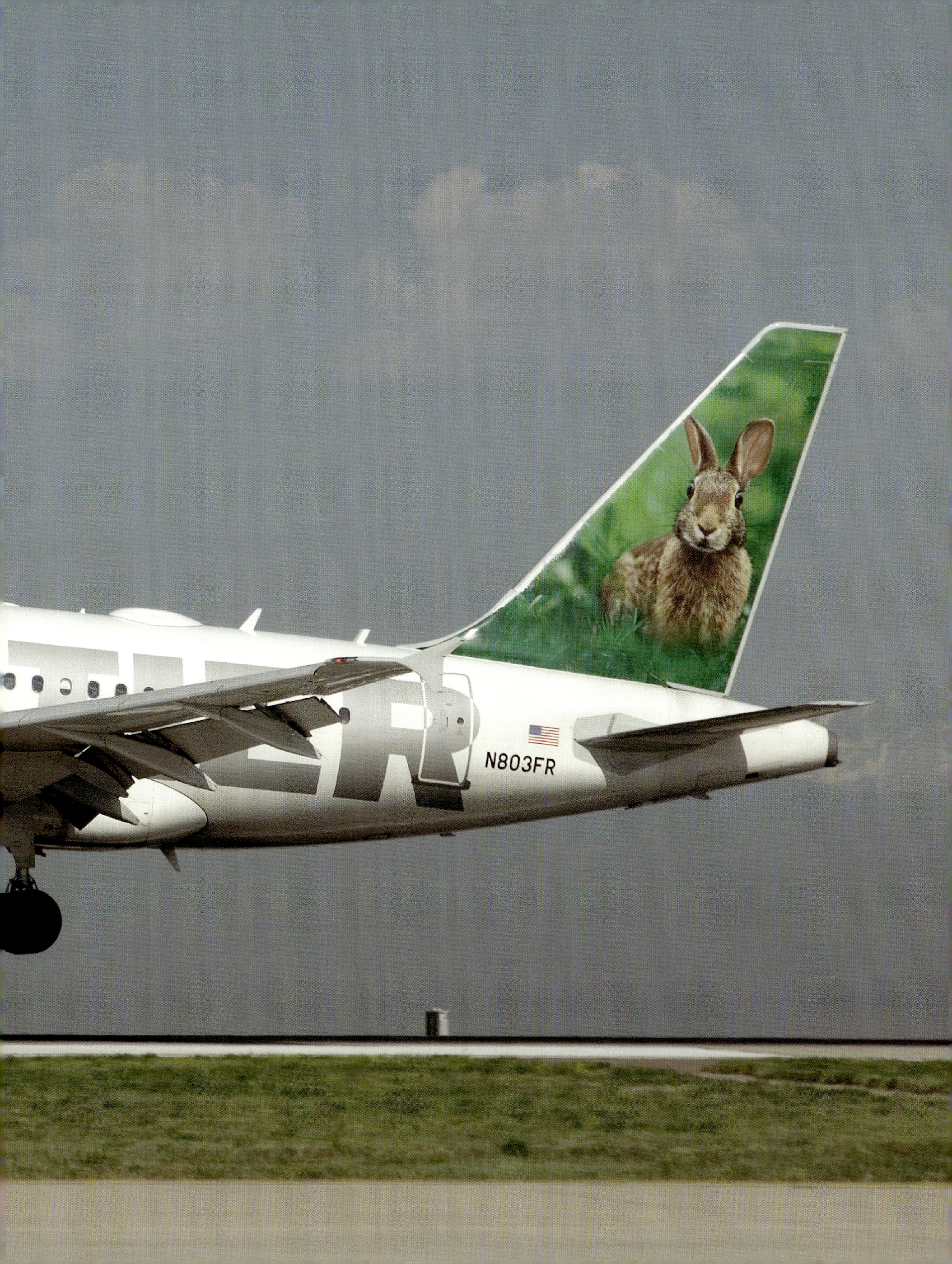
N803FR

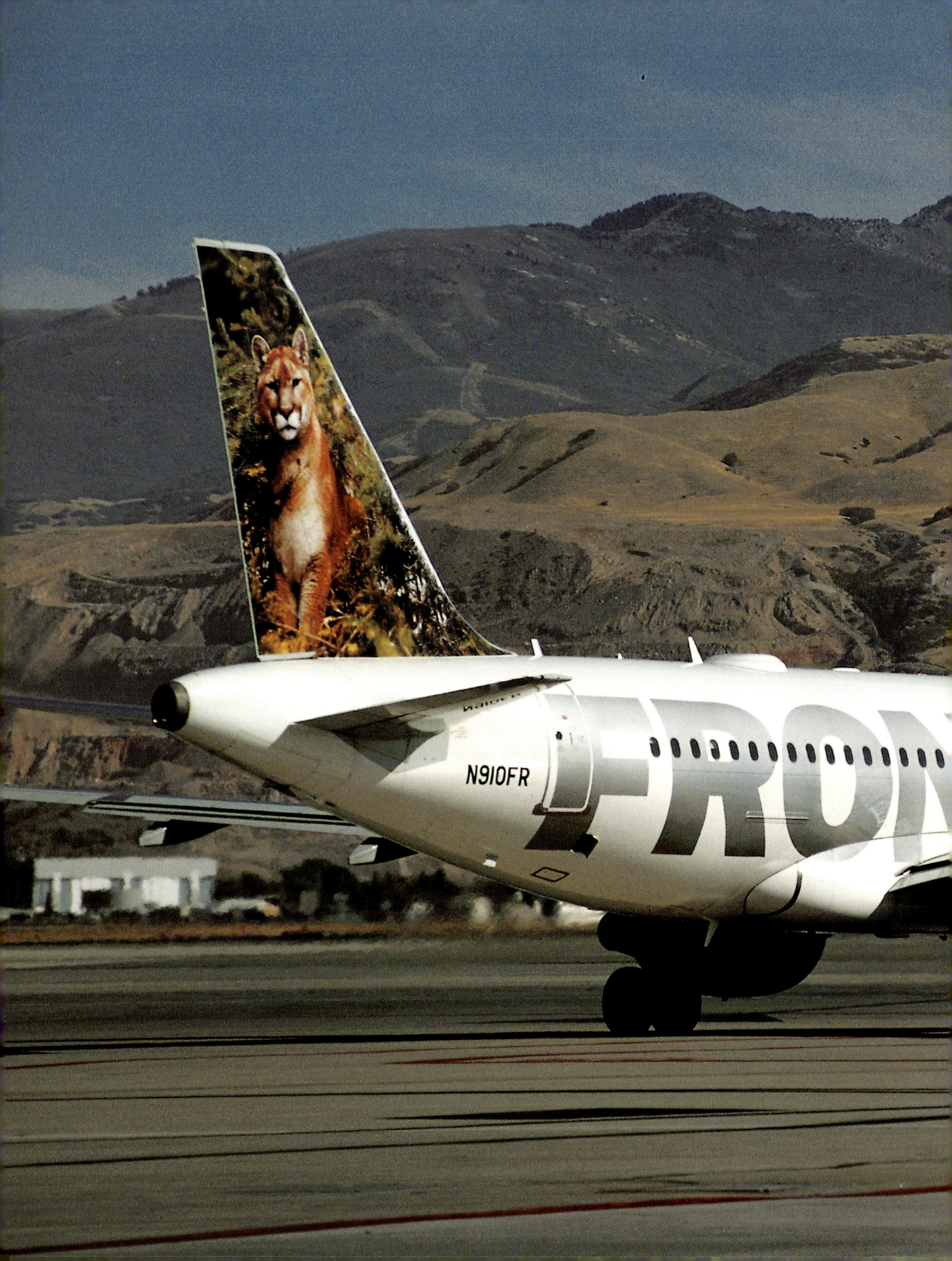
N910FR
FRON

A whole different animal.

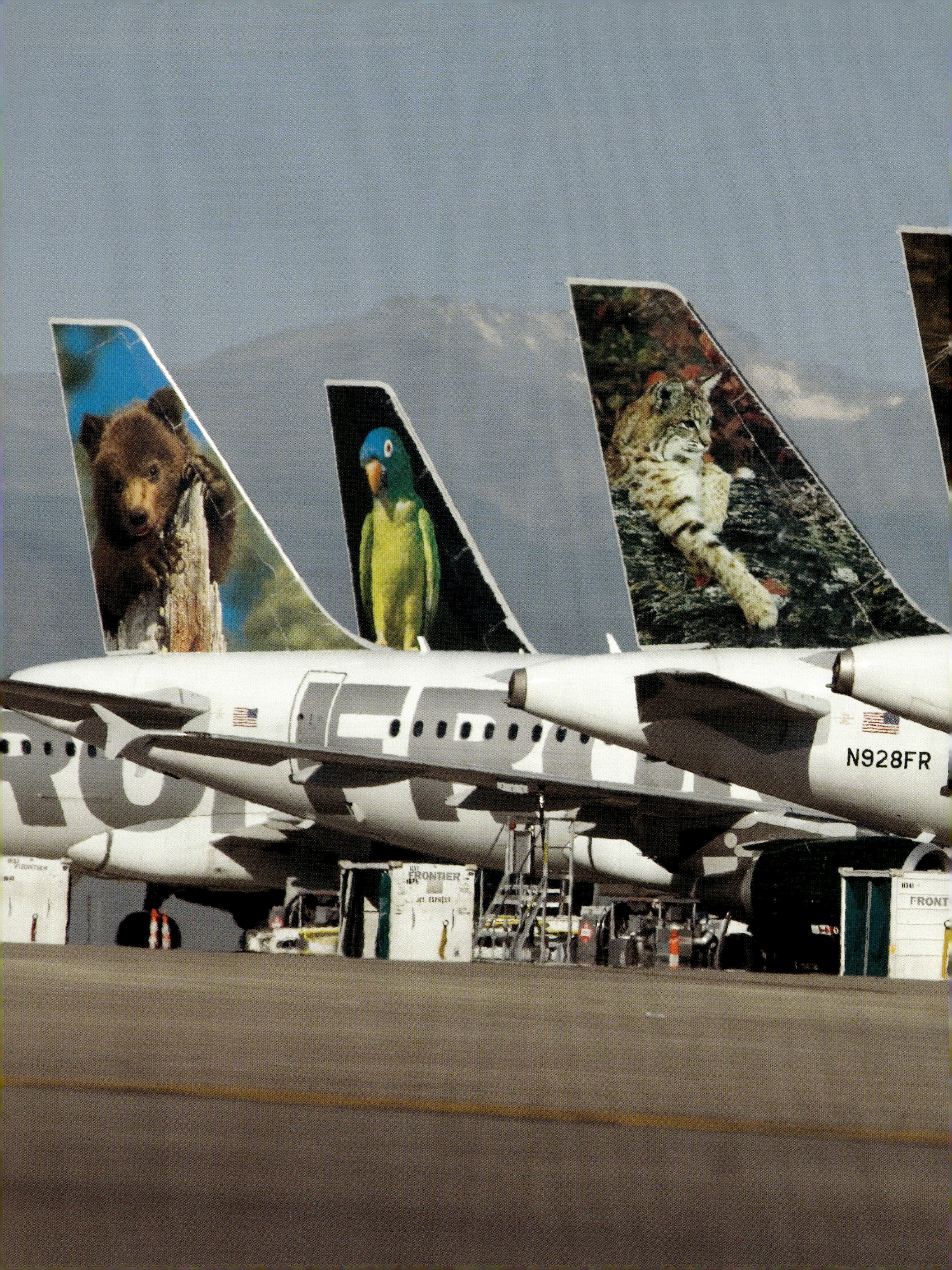
N928FR
FRONTIER
FRONT

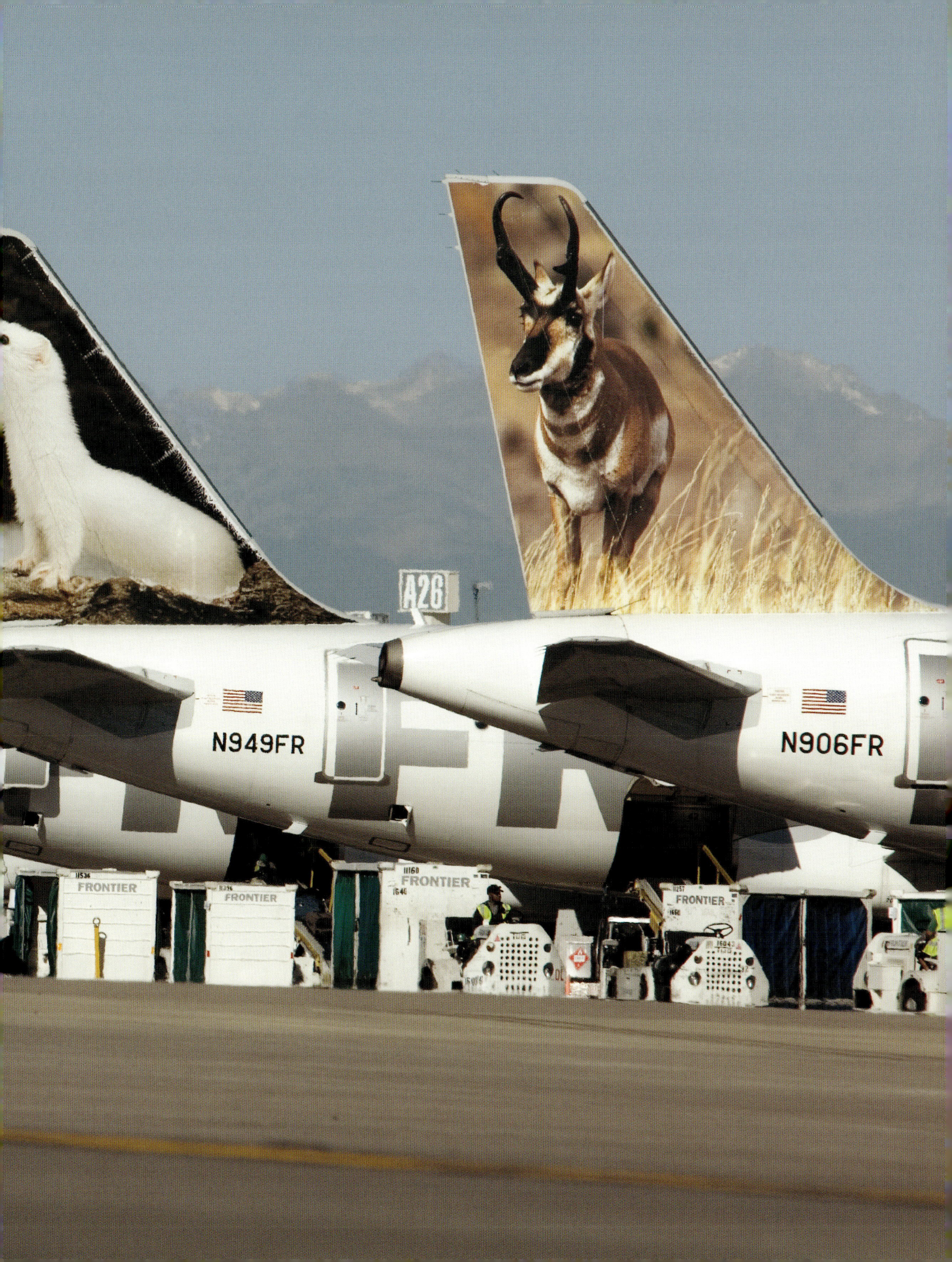
A26
N949FR
N906FR
FRONTIER
FRONTIER
FRONTIER
FRONTIER

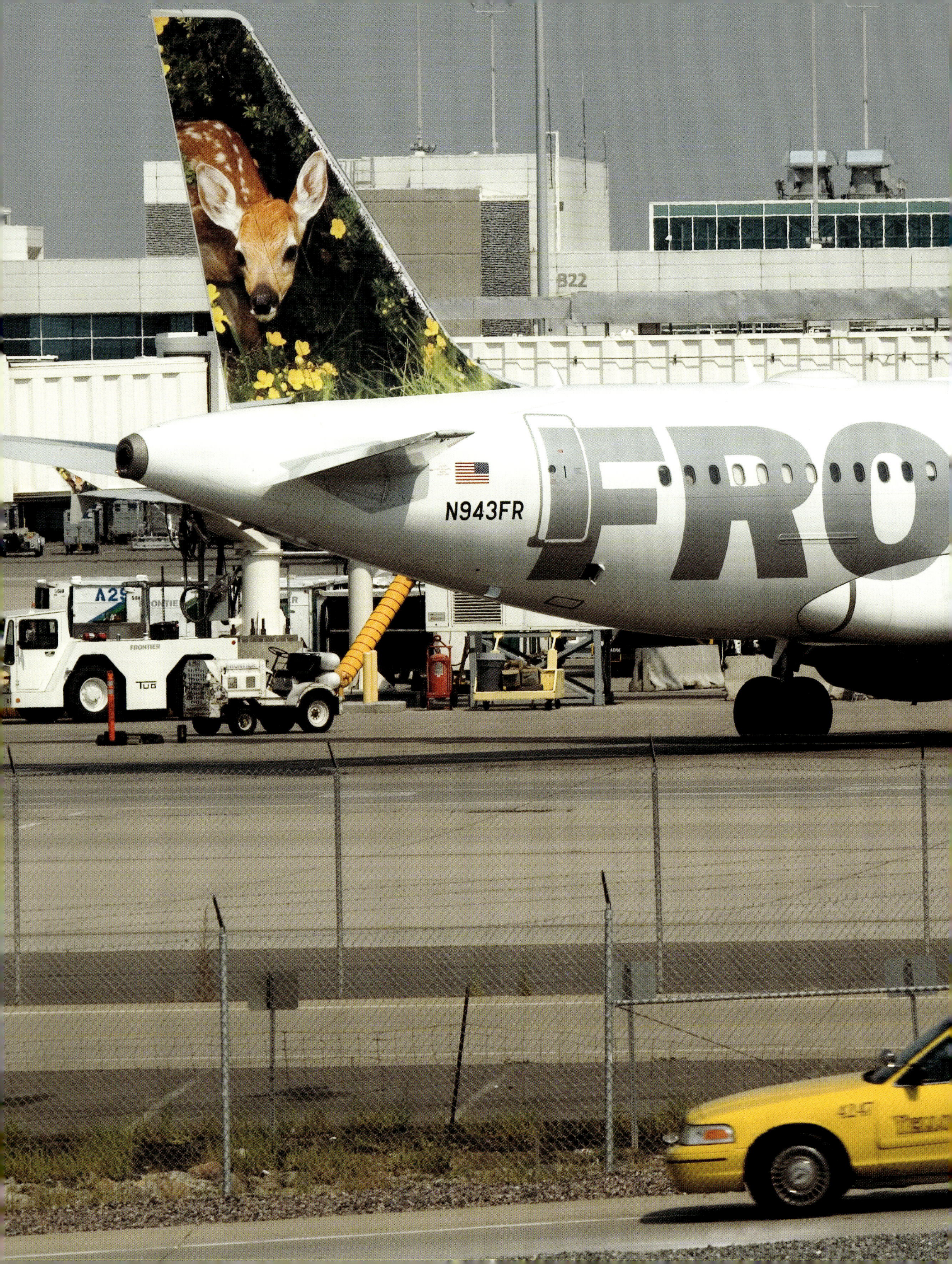
B22
N943FR
FRO
FRONTIER
TUG

A whole different animal.

A26

FRONTIER

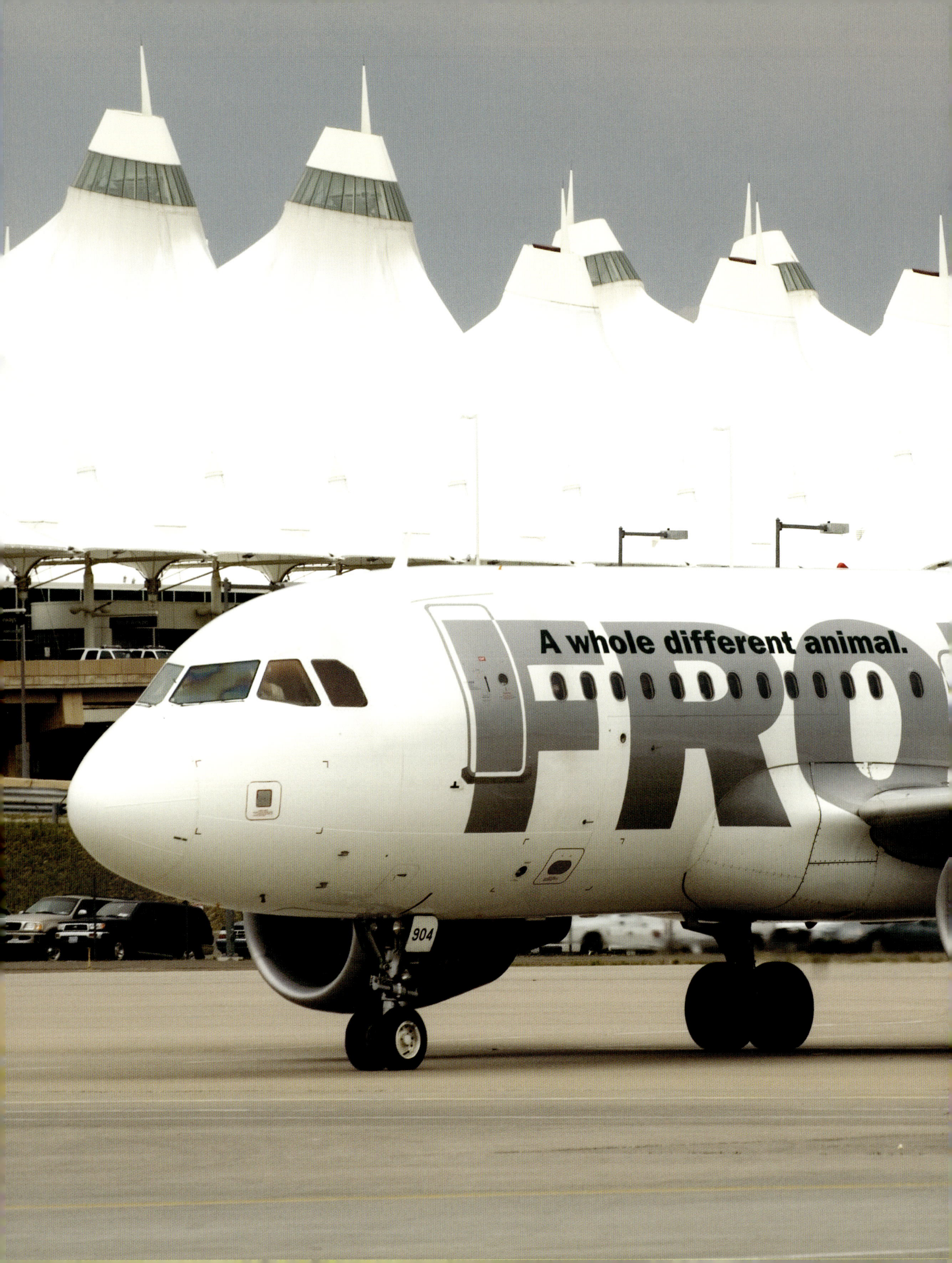
A whole different animal.
FRO
904

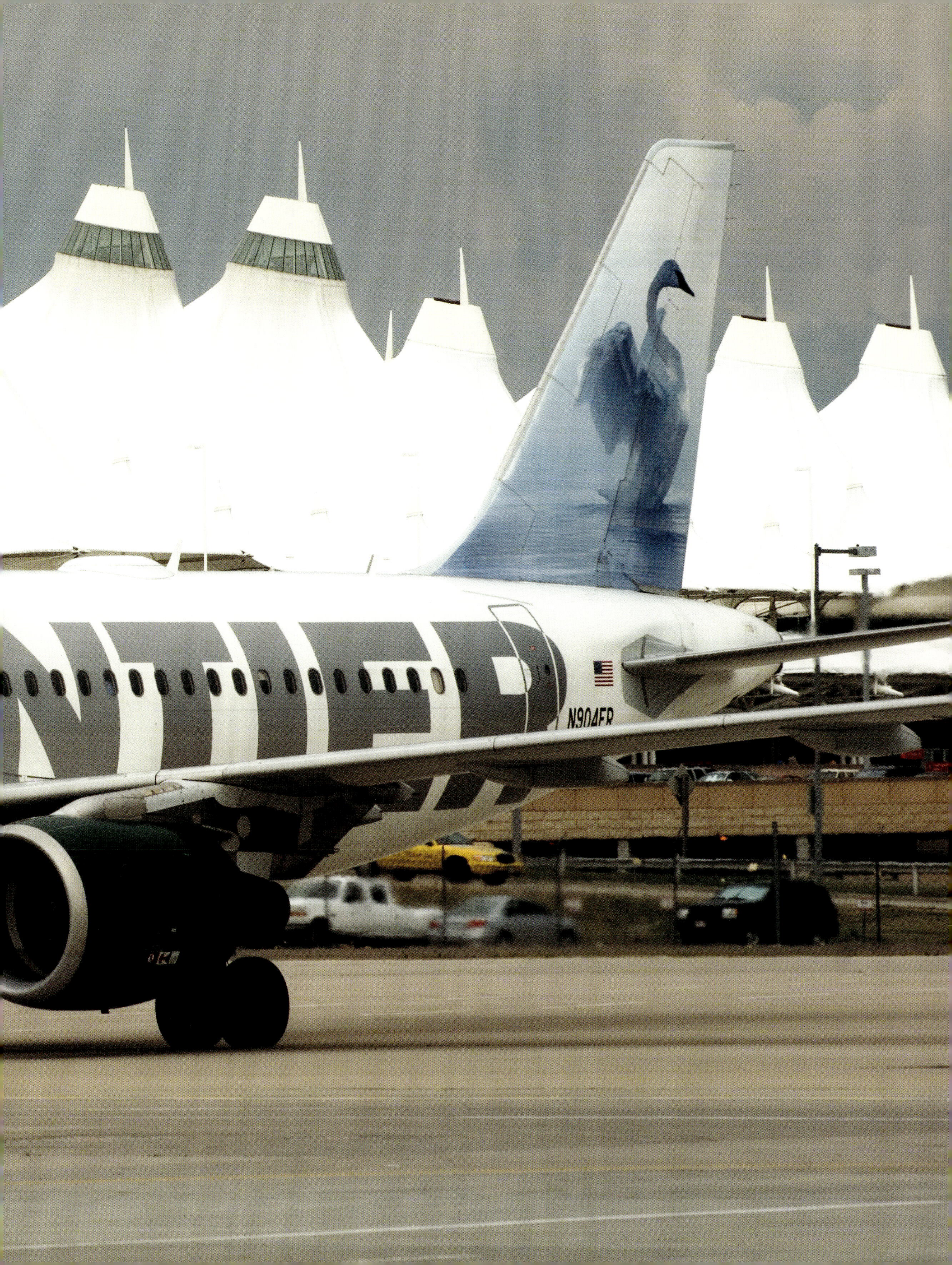
N904FR

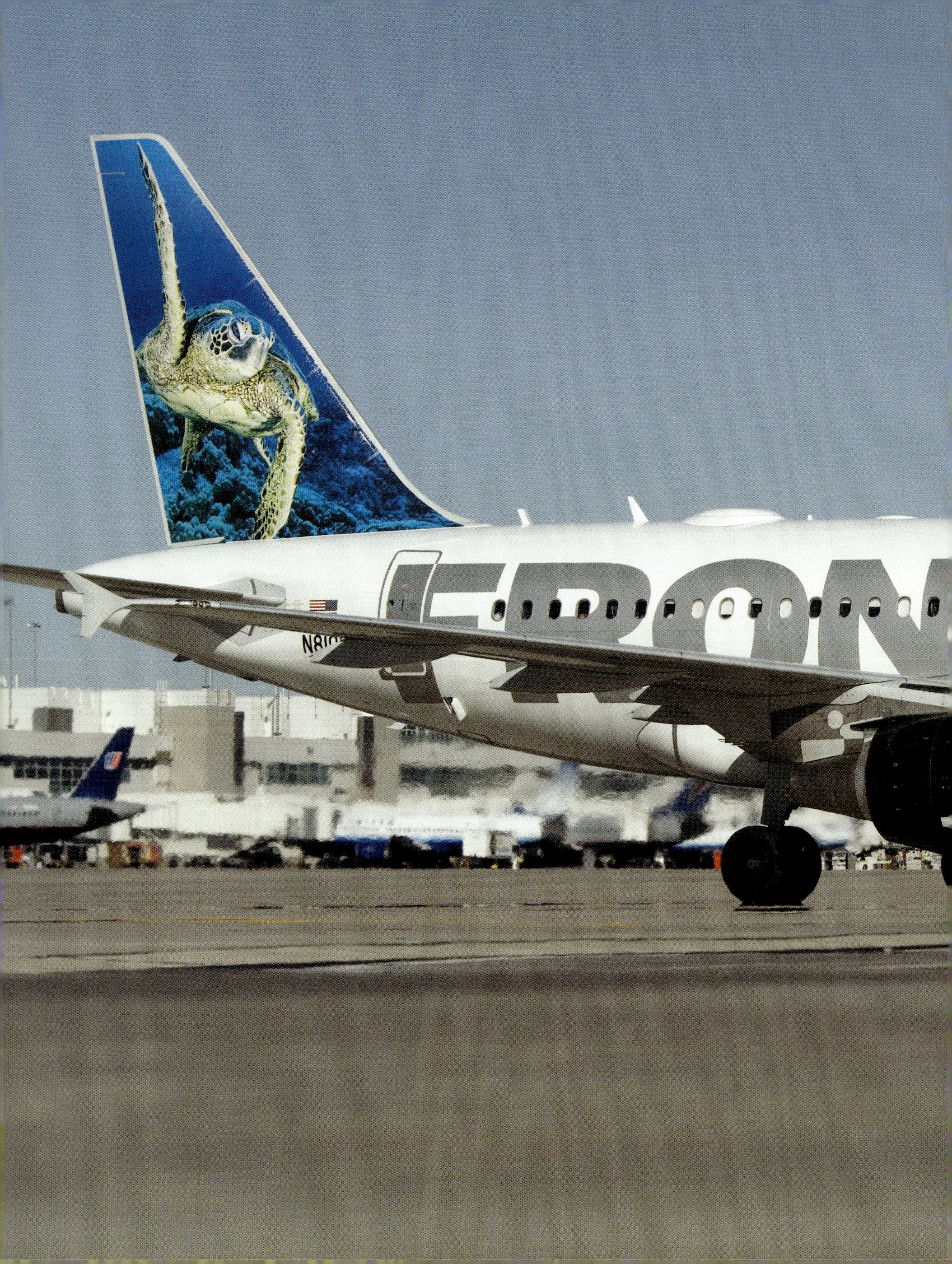

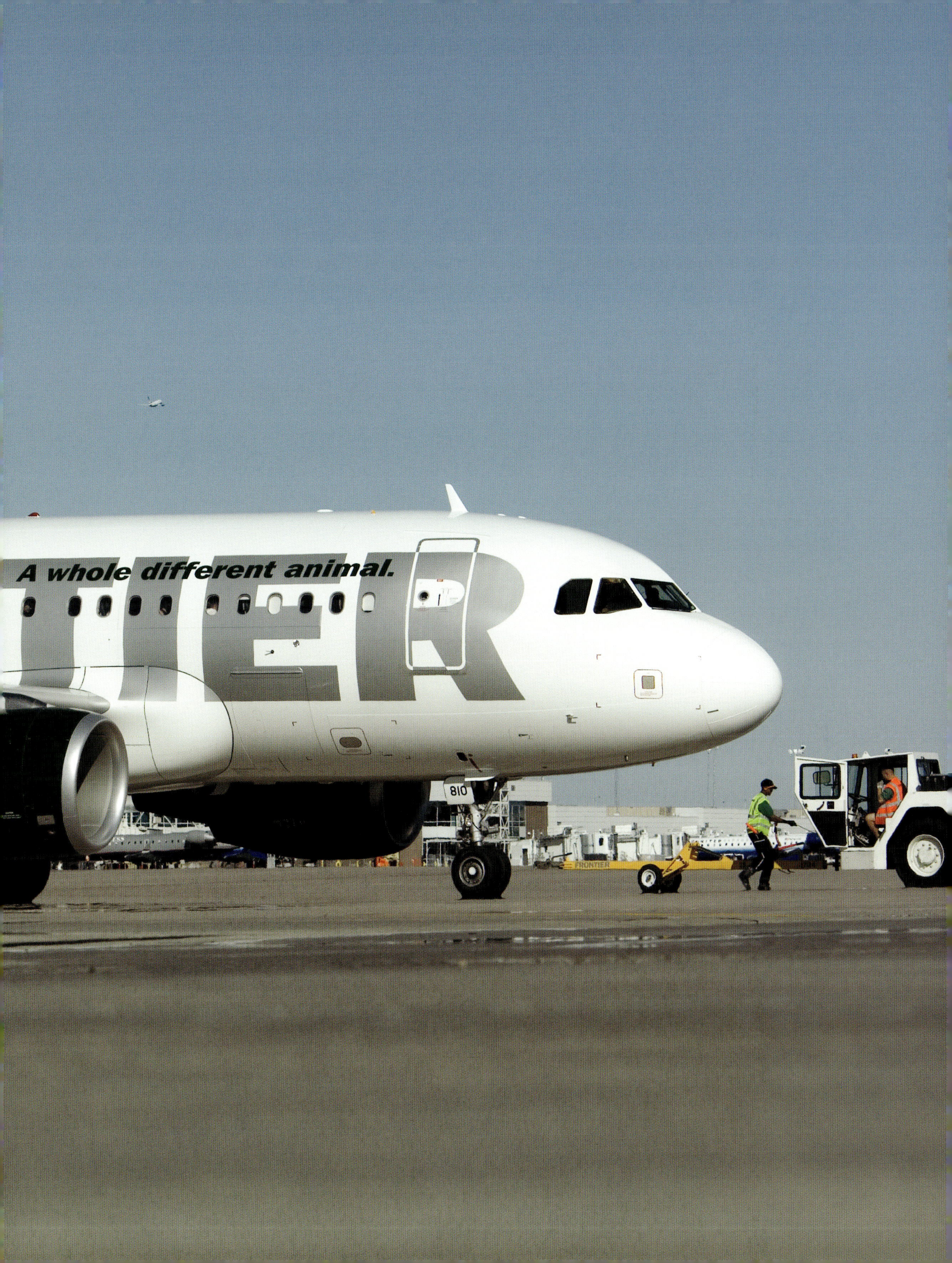

A whole different animal.
TIER
810
FRONTIER

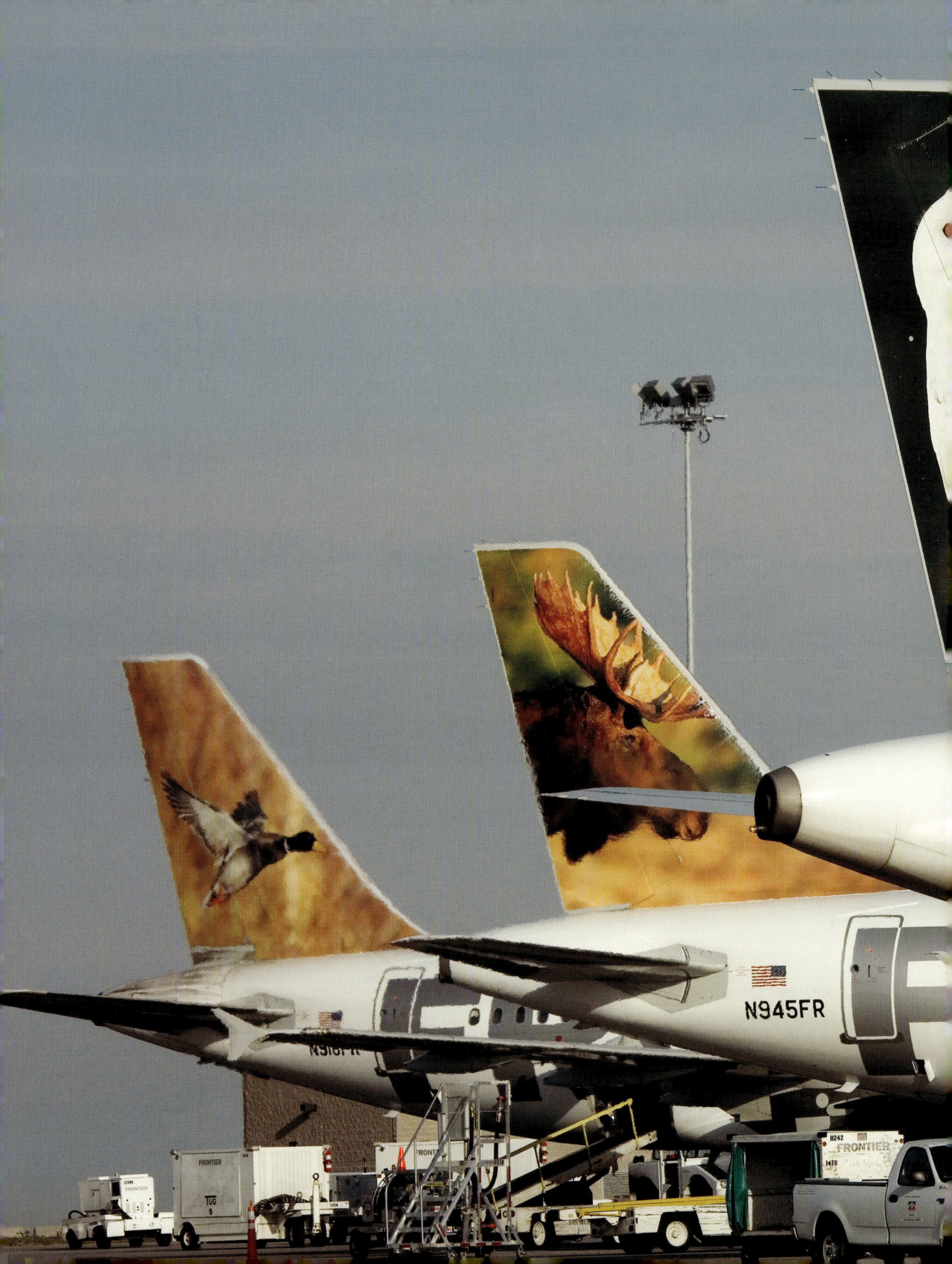
N945FR
FRONTIER

N917FR

A whole different animal.

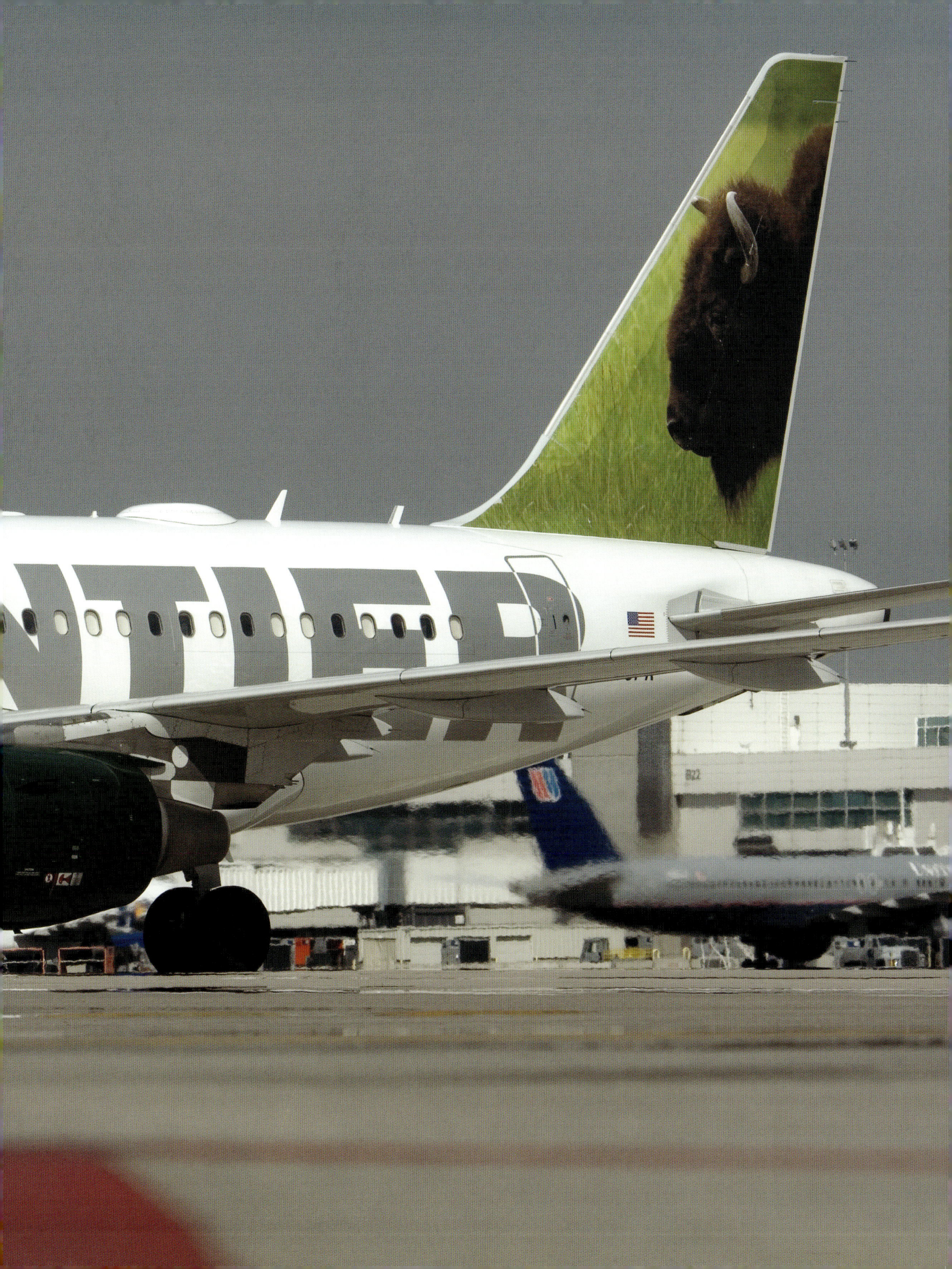

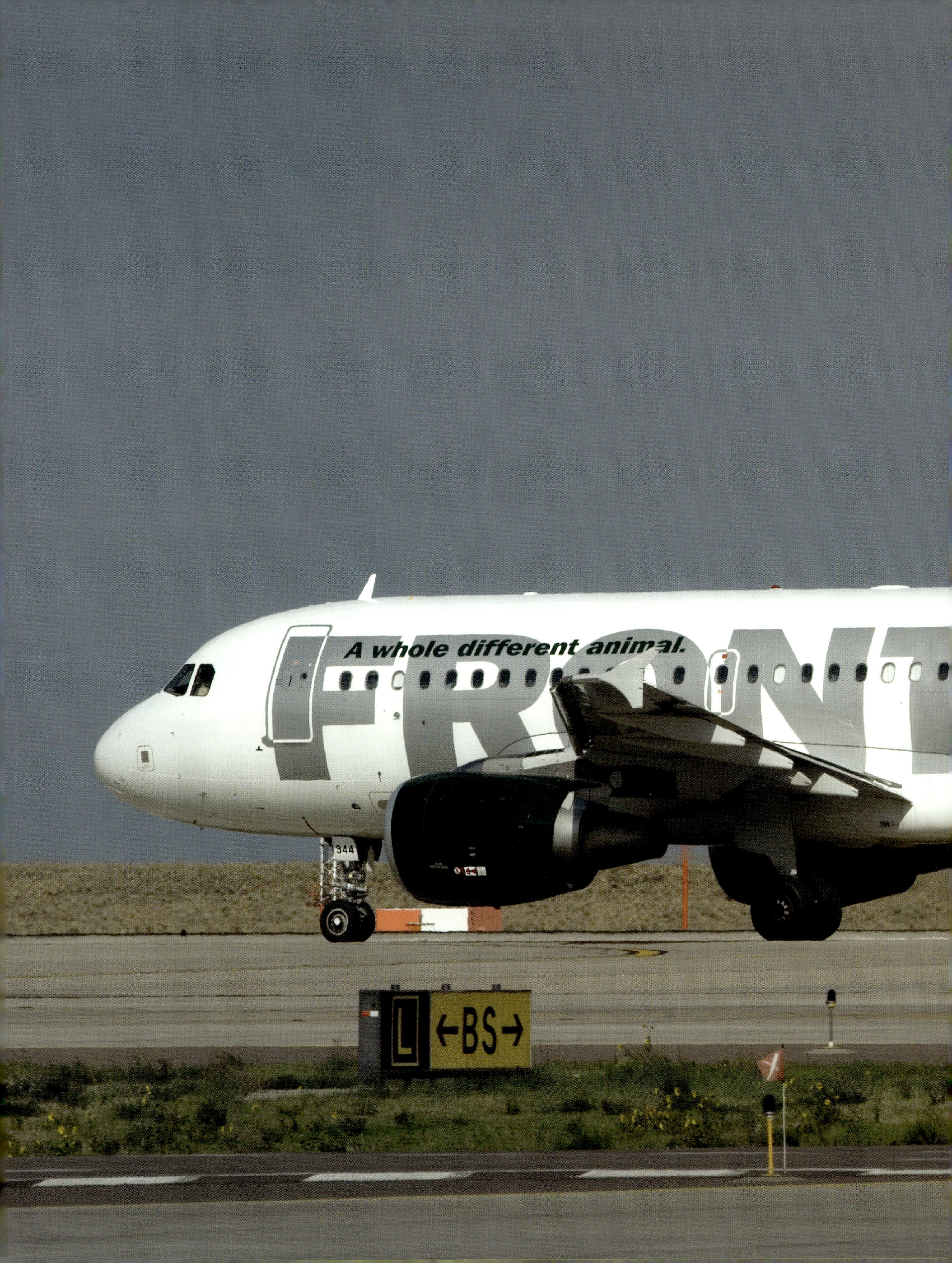
A whole different animal.
FRONT
944
L
←BS→

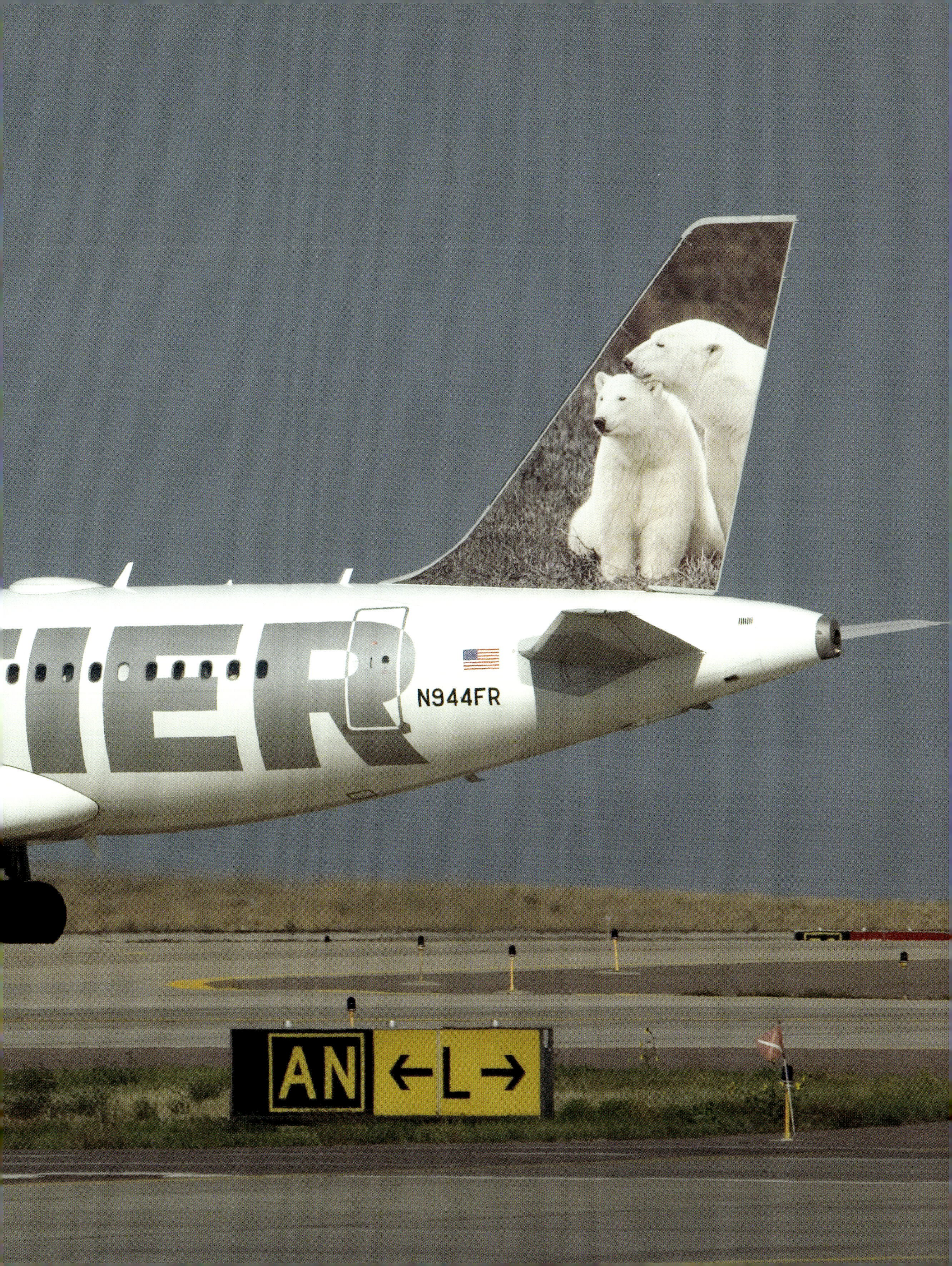
IER
N944FR
AN
L

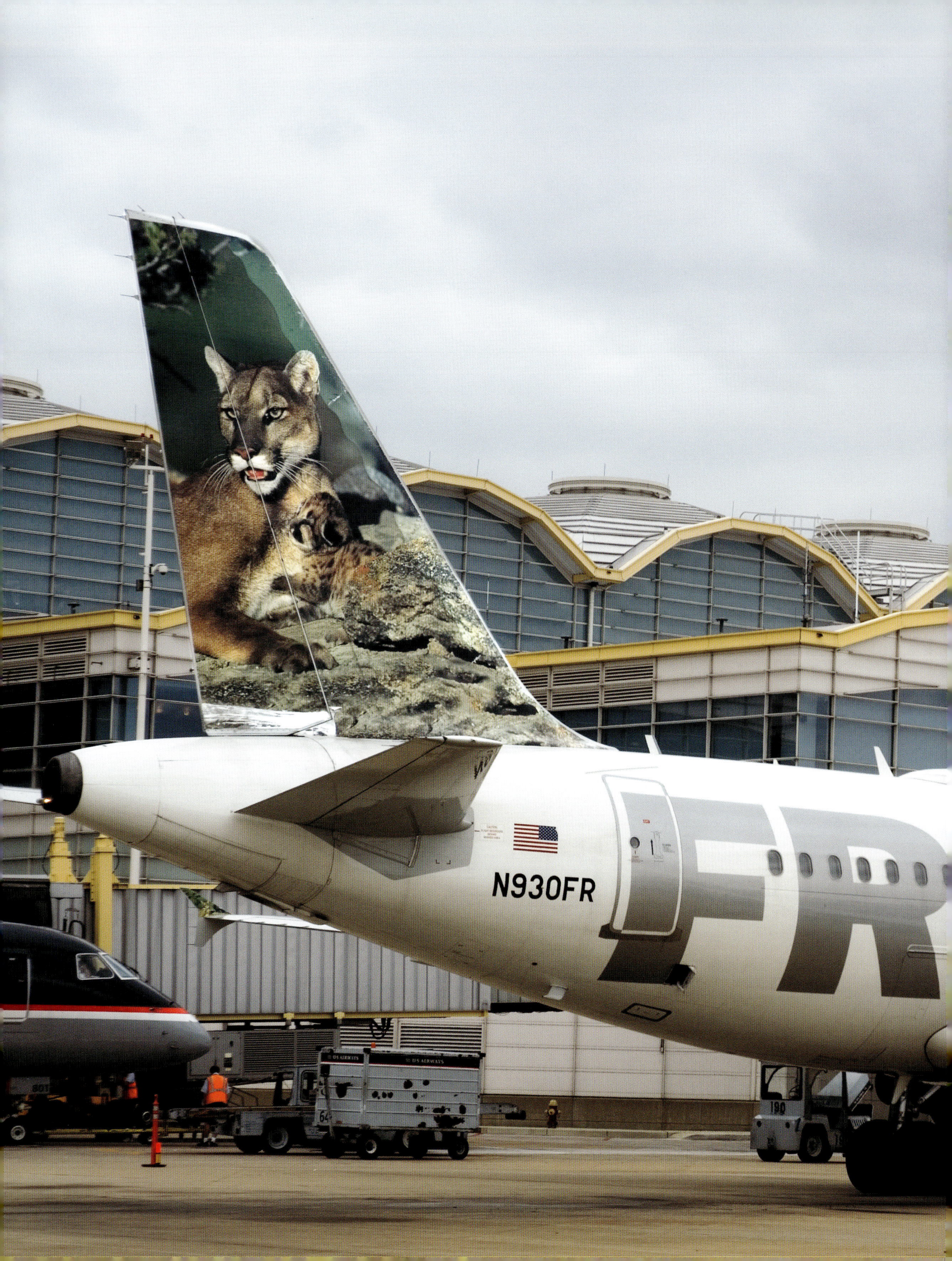
N930FR
FR

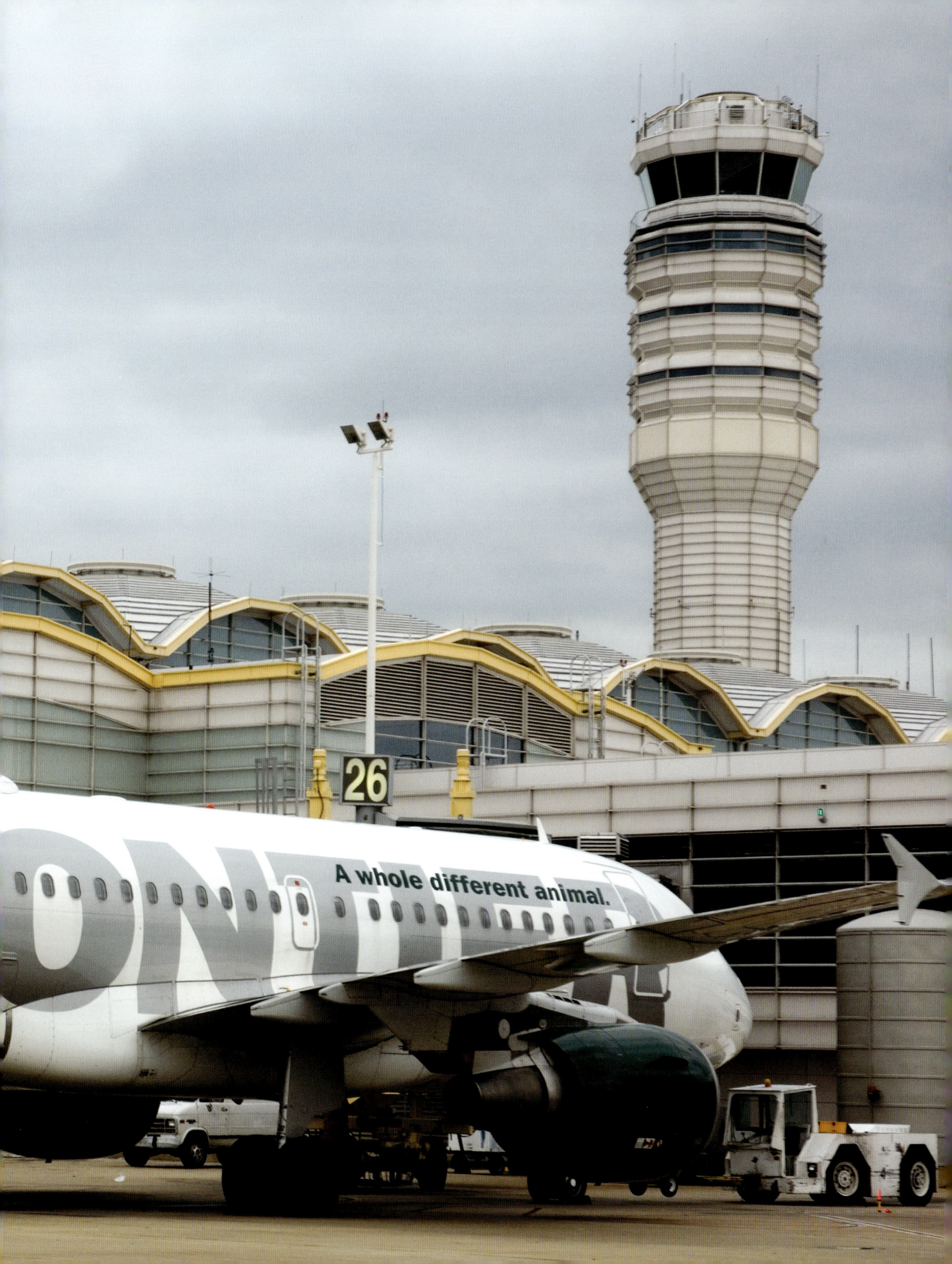
26
A whole different animal.

A whole different animal.

N942FR

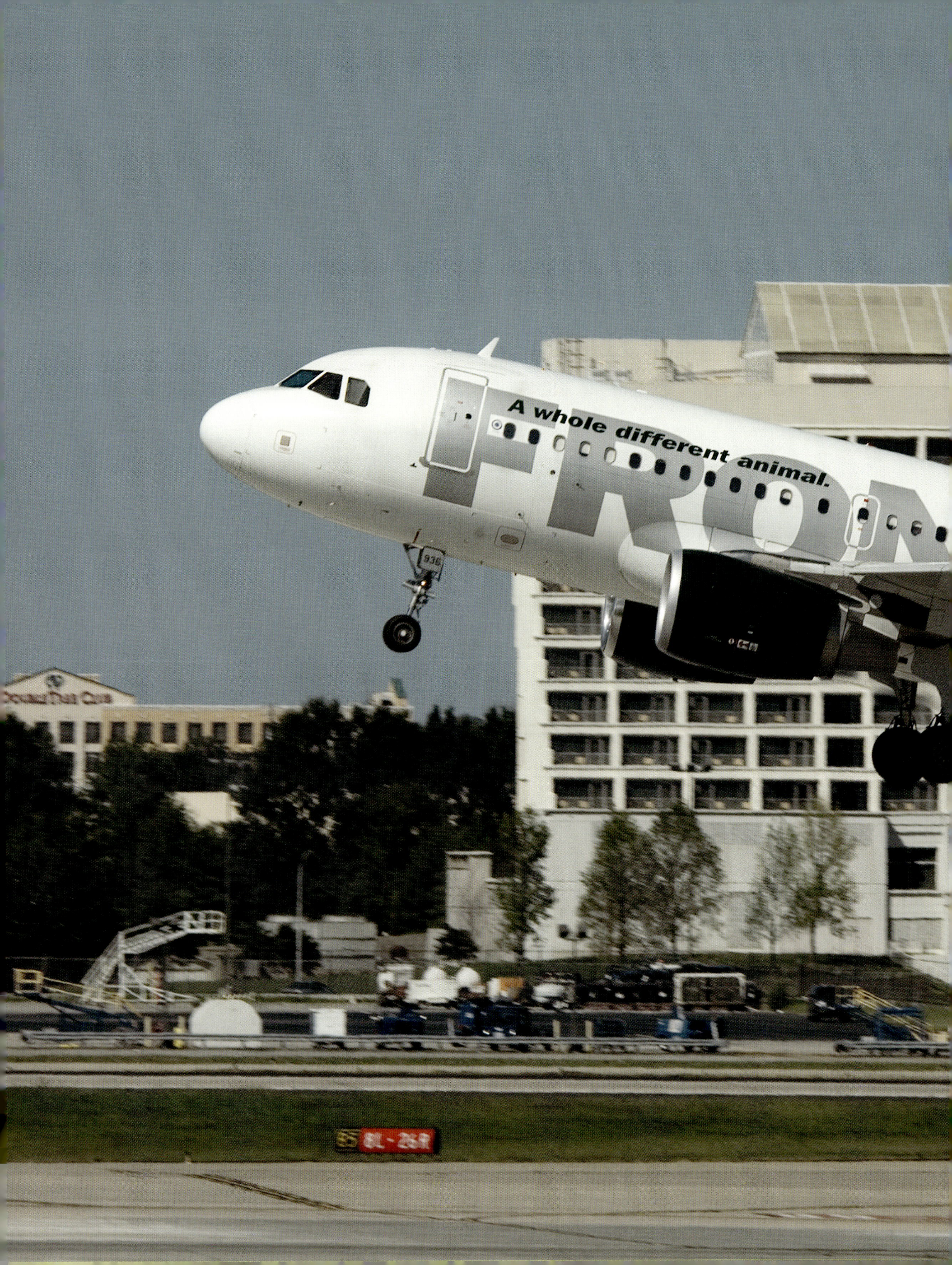
A whole different animal.
FRON
8L - 26R

RENAISSANCE HOTEL

N936FR

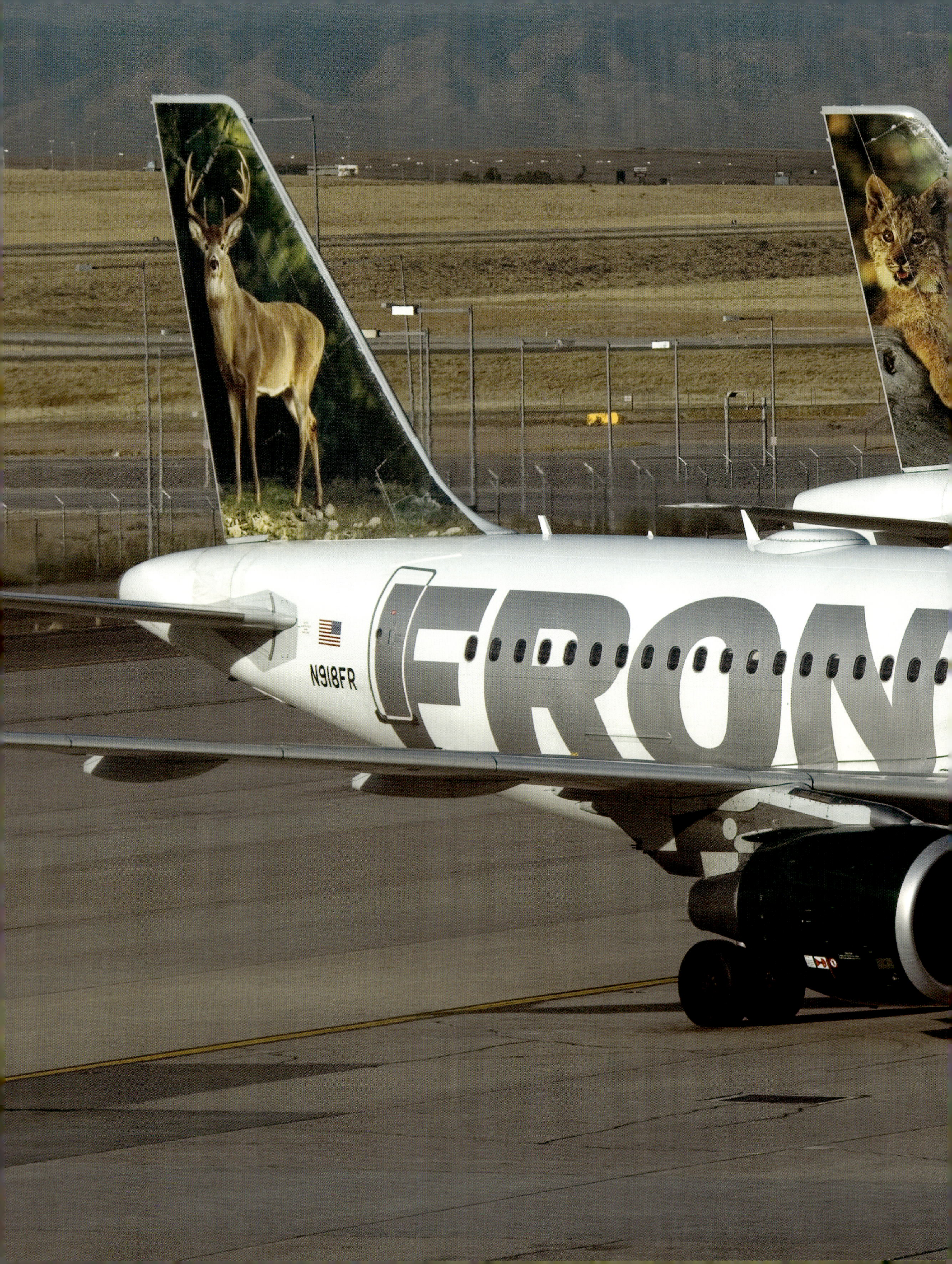
FRON
N918FR

A whole different animal.

42 Ft.

A whole different animal.

Tail Clearance Ht.   42 Ft.

N923FR

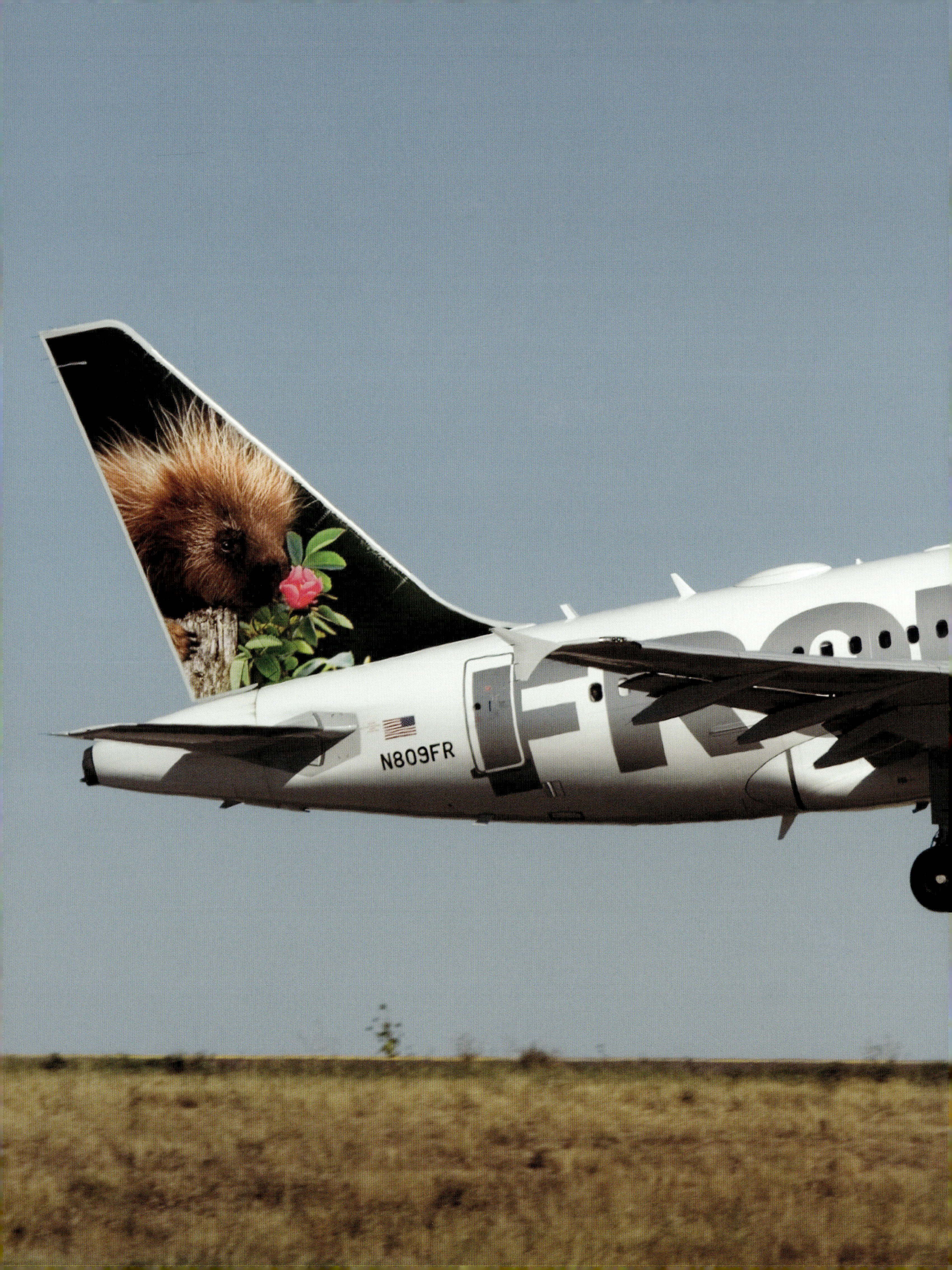
N809FR

A whole different animal.

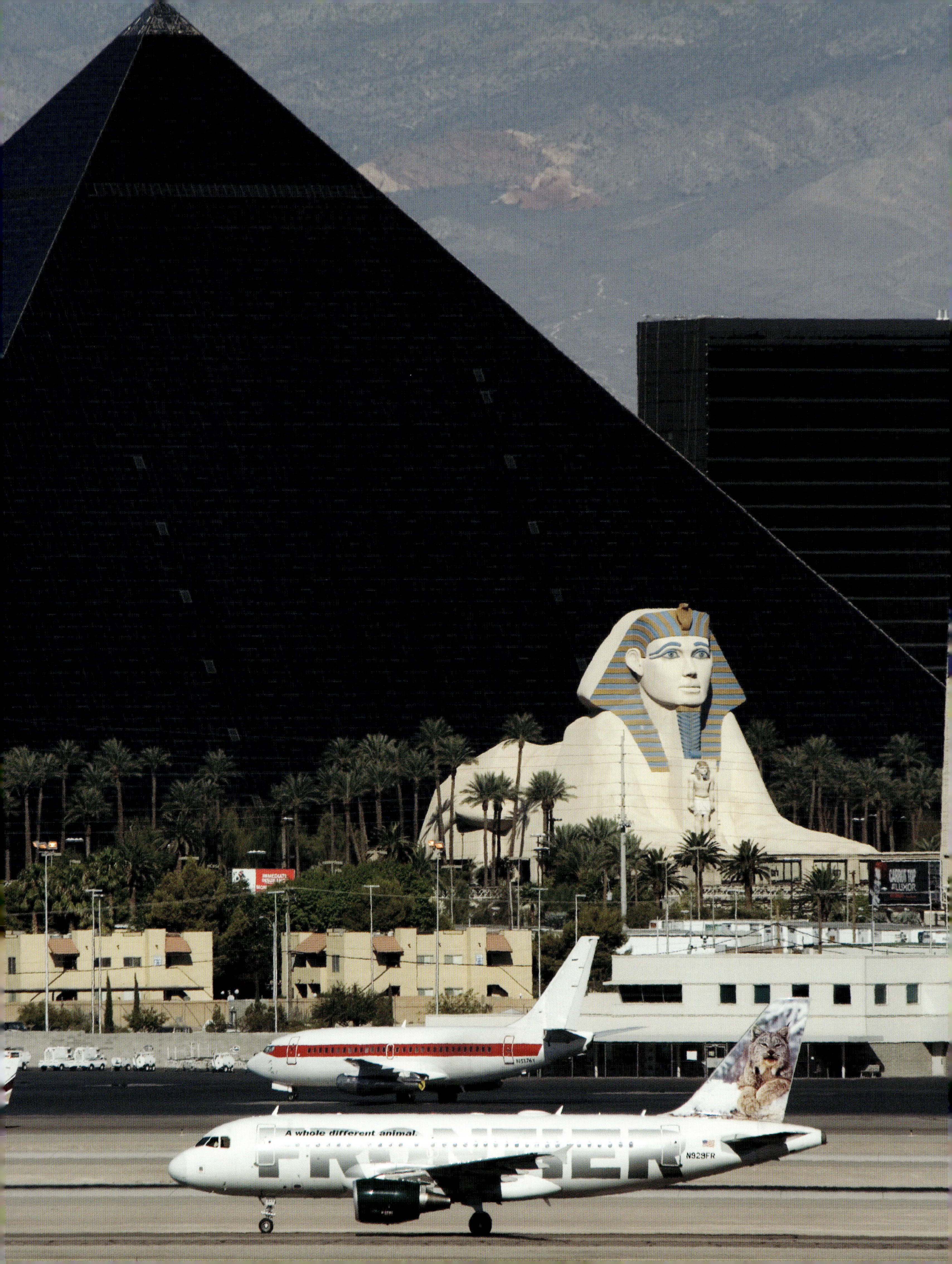
A whole different animal.
FRONTIER
N929FR

Das Streckennetz
Network Map

Die Tiere – *The Animals*

N801FR	Airbus A318	**Grizwald – Grizzlybär/Grizzly Bear**
N802FR	Airbus A318	**Montana – Waipiti/ Elk**
N803FR	Airbus A318	**Stu – FLorida Waldkaninchen/Eastern Cottontail**
N804FR	Airbus A318	**Mo & Jo – Rotfuchswelpen/Red Fox Pups**
N805FR	Airbus A318	**Ollie – Bartkauz/Great Gray Owl**
N806FR	Airbus A318	**Humphrey – Amerikanischer Bison/American Bison**
N807FR	Airbus A318	**Charlie – Berglöwe/Cougar**
N808FR	Airbus A318	**Clover -Rehkitz/Fawn**
N809FR	Airbus A318	**Spike – Stachelschwein/Porcupine**
N810FR	Airbus A318	**Sheldon – Meeresschildkröte/Sea Turtle**
N812FR	Airbus A318	**Grizzlybär/Grizzly Bear**
N901FR	Airbus A319	**Wally – Wolf/Gray Wolf**
N902FR	Airbus A319	**Woody – Brautente/Wood Duck**
N903FR	Airbus A319	**Ozzy – Killerwal/Orca**
N904FR	Airbus A319	**Grace – Trompeterschwan/Trumpeter Swan**
N905FR	Airbus A319	**Sherman – Seehund/Seal**
N906FR	Airbus A319	**Andy – Gabelbock/Pronghorn**
N907FR	Airbus A319	**Mel – Maultierhirsch/Mule Deer**
N908FR	Airbus A319	**Holly – Kanadareiher/Great Blue Heron**
N909FR	Airbus A319	**Lucy – Kanadagans/Canadian Goose**
N910FR	Airbus A319	**Sal – Berglöwe/Cougar Sal**
N912FR	Airbus A319	**Trixie – Rotfuchswelpe/Red Fox Pup**
N913FR	Airbus A319	**Hamilton – Kolibri/Hummingbird**
N914FR	Airbus A319	**Stretch – Silberreiher/Great Egret**
N915FR	Airbus A319	**Sally – Mustang**
N916FR	Airbus A319	**O'Malley – Stockente/Mallard**
N917FR	Airbus A319	**Doc – Schneeeule/Snowy Owl**
N918FR	Airbus A319	**Jake – Weißwedelhirsch/White Tailed Deer**
N919FR	Airbus A319	**Lance – Ozelot/Ocelot**
N920FR	Airbus A319	**Carl – Kojote/Coyote**

N921FR	Airbus A319	Fritz – Schneeziege/Mountain Goat		N936FR	Airbus A319	Earl – Walross/Walrus
N922FR	Airbus A319	Foxy – Rotfuchs/Red Fox		N937FR	Airbus A319	Carmen – Blaukopfsittich/Blue Crowned Conure
N923FR	Airbus A319	Rudy – Waschbär/Raccoon		N938FR	Airbus A319	Misty – Polarfuchs/Arctic Fox Misty
N924FR	Airbus A319	Klondike & Snow – Eisbärenjunge/Polar Bear Cubs		N939Fr	Airbus A319	Jim, Joe, Jay, Gary – Kaiserpinguin/Emperor Penguins
N925FR	Airbus A319	Dale – Alaska-Schneeschaf/Dall's Sheep		N940FR	Airbus A319	Jack – Schneeschuhhase/Snowshoe Hare
N926FR	Airbus A319	Domino – Schwarzwedelwild/Black Tailed Deer Fawn		N941FR	Airbus A319	Lobo – Wolf/Gray Wolf
N927FR	Airbus A319	Flip – Großer Tümmler/Bottle Nosed Dolphin		N942FR	Airbus A319	Stanley – Dickhornschaf/Bighorn Sheep
N928FR	Airbus A319	Hank – Rotluchs/Bobcat		N943FR	Airbus A319	Cloe – Rehkitz/Deer Fawn
N929FR	Airbus A319	Larry – Kanadischer Luchs/Lynx		N944FR	Airbus A319	Alberta & Clipper – Eisbär/Polar Bear & Cub
N930FR	Airbus A319	Lola & Max – Berglöwin mit Jungem/Cougar & Cub		N945FR	Airbus A319	Chocolate – Elch/Moose
N931FR	Airbus A319	Jo-Jo – Amerikanische Schwarzbären/Black Bear Cub		N946FR	Airbus A319	Perry – Hornlund/Puffin
N932FR	Airbus A319	Sarge – Weißkopfseeadler/Bald Eagle		N947FR	Airbus A319	Maya – Jaguar
N933FR	Airbus A319	Sebastian – Königsbussard/Ferruginous Hawk		N948FR	Airbus A319	Pete – Pelikan/Pelican
N934FR	Airbus A319	L.J. – Kanadisches Luchsjunge/Lynx Kitten		N949FR	Airbus A319	Erma – Hermelin/Ermine
N935FR	Airbus A319	Hector – Seeotter/Sea Otter		N950FR	Airbus A319	Bob – Delfin/Dolphin

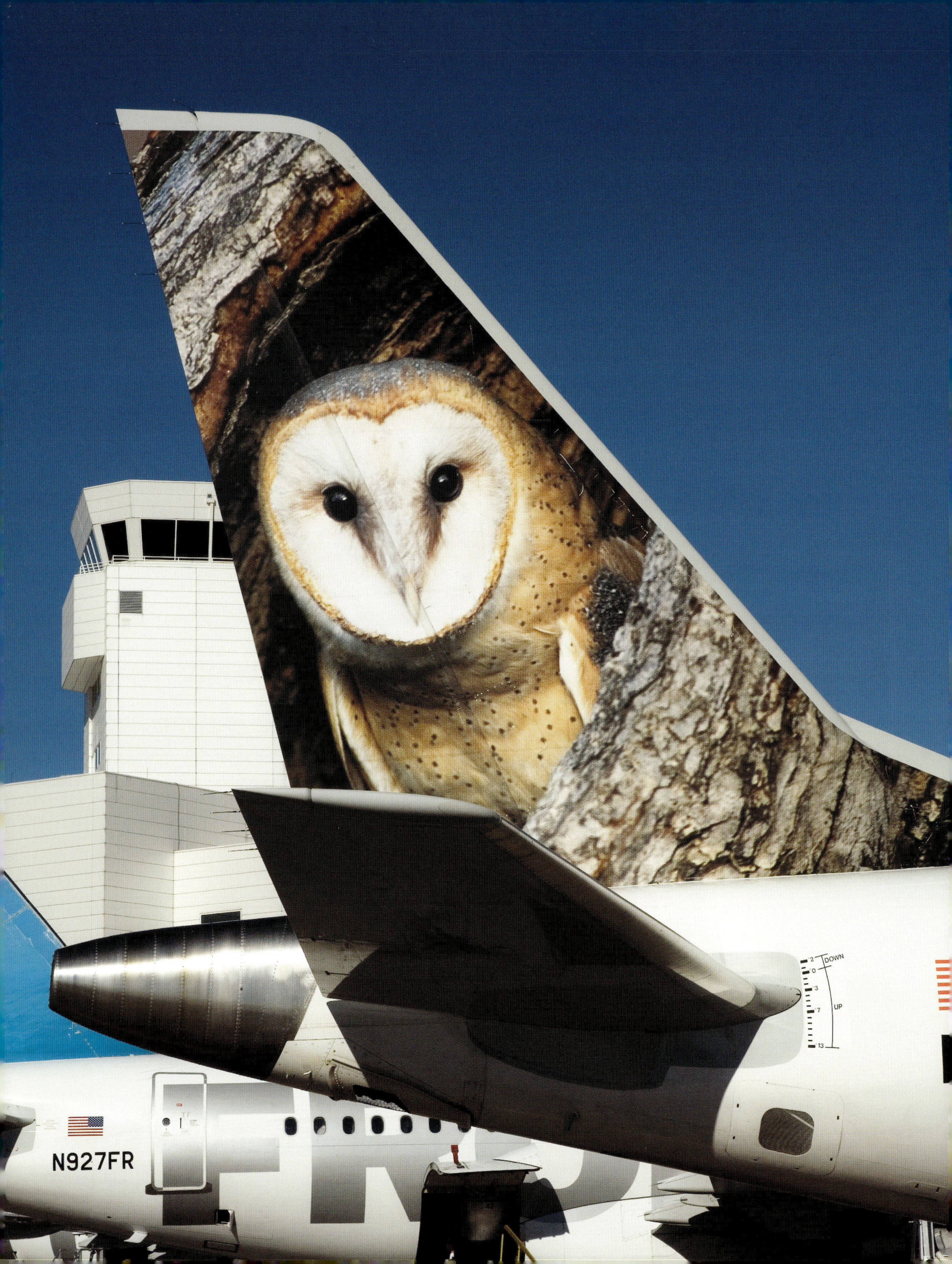
N927FR
DOWN
UP

Frontier Express

Frontiers Töchter · *Frontier's subsidiaries*

Wie viele Fluggesellschaften, erweitert auch Frontier Airlines seinen Aktionsradius durch Partnerschaften. Seit 2001 ist der Regional-Carrier Great Lakes Aviation auch im Auftrag von Frontier unterwegs – mit Embraer Turboprops für 30 Fluggäste und 19-sitzige Raytheon Beachcraft-Flugzeugen zu insgesamt 35 regionalen Zielen. Im Januar 2007 schloss die „tierische Airline" einen Elf-Jahres-Vertrag mit Republic Airlines ab, die unter dem Namen Frontier JetExpress die 43 Flughäfen in elf US-Staaten anfliegen. JetExpress setzt 17 Flugzeuge vom 76-Sitzer Embraer 170 ein.

Lynx Aviation wird die jüngste Frontier Tochter heißen. Die Geburt sollte ursprünglich im Herbst 2007 sein, verspätete sich aber auf Grund administrativer Verzögerungen. Mit zehn Bombardier Q400-Flugzeugen soll der Frontier-Abkömmling eine Reihe von kleineren regionalen Zielorten bedienen, vor allem in den Rocky Mountains. Auf dem Seitenleitwerk des ersten Bombardier-Turboprop prangt bereits das Wappentier der Frontier-Tochter: Luchsbaby „Larry".

Just like many other airlines, Frontier is constantly extending its radius of action by means of partnerships. Frontier Airlines have been contracting with regional carrier Great Lakes Aviation since 2001. Great Lakes operate 19-seat Raytheon Beachcraft as well as 30-seat Embraer turboprop aircraft to as many as 35 destinations. In January 2007, the 'beastly' airline put pen to paper on an eleven-year contract with Republic Airlines to serve 43 destinations in eleven U.S. States. This service, operating as Frontier JetExpress, runs a fleet of 17 76-seat Embreaer 170.

Lynx Aviation will be the latest Frontier offspring. The company was scheduled to be established in autumn 2007. However, the company's inauguration had to be postponed over administrative delays. Lynx is to serve a series of minor regional destinations, particularly in the Rocky Mountain Range with its ten Bombardier Q400 aircraft. The Frontier subsidiary's first Bombardier turboprop displays the company's heraldic beast: Larry-the-Kitten-Lynx.

Mit 17 Flugzeugen vom Typ Embraer 170 fliegt Frontier JetExpress 43 Airports in elf amerikanischen Staaten an. Auf diesen Routen rechnet sich der Einsatz des kleinsten Airbus, der A318, nicht.

Frontier JetExpress run 17 Embraer 170 aircraft to 43 destinations in eleven U.S. States. Operating A318, the smallest Airbus type, is inefficient on these routes.

Die Flugzeuge
Aircraft

A318 und A319 – die "Benjamine" der Airbus-Familie

Die A319 und die A318 sind die jüngsten und kleinsten Mitglieder der Standardrumpf-Familie von Airbus, der Flugzeuge mit nur einem Gang in der Kabine (Single Aisle). Ihre direkten Geschwister sind die 150-sitzige A320 sowie die gestretchte Variante A321 für 185 Passagiere.

„Familienmutter" A320 ist seit gut 20 Jahren in der Luft unterwegs. Ihren Erstflug hatte sie am 22. Februar 1987. Die A320, die bis zu 180 Passagiere maximal 5700 Kilometer weit befördern kann, ist mit über 3000 bestellten Maschinen der „Bestseller" der gesamten Airbus-Familie.

Nach ihrem Erstflug am 25. August 1995 nahm die A319 am

A318 & A319: Benjamins in the Airbus family

A318 and A319 are the youngest and smallest members of the Airbus family with a standard fuselage (the so-called single-aisle aircraft). Its immediate relatives are the A320 and its stretched version A321 with a capacity of 150 and 185 passengers respectively.

The family's mother would be A320 which has been in the skies for 20 years. The A320 first flew on 22 February 1987. This aircraft, carrying a maximum of 180 passengers for a distance of 3,078 NM, can well be referred to as the best-seller of the entire Airbus product range, recording well over 3,000 orders.

After its maiden flight on 25 August 1995, a type A319 aircraft was first run on scheduled services on 30 April 1996 with Swissair. Type A319 aircraft are some 13 ft shorter than A320s, conveying 124 to 145 passengers.

Its smaller sister A318 was first delivered to Frontier Airlines on 21 July 2003 featuring a grizzly bear on its tail. The 100-seat Airbus aircraft completed its maiden flight on 15 January 2002. It is designed to carry 107 to 129 passengers.

A319 aircraft are powered by CFM56-5 or Rolls Royce V2500A5 engines. The A318 series comes with Pratt & Whitney PW6000 or CFM56-5B engines. Cruising speed for aircraft in the A320 family is 0.78 Mo.

All aircraft in the A320 family share a sufficient number of properties to allow operation as a single aircraft type. The following parameters are absolutely identical throughout the series: cockpit, flying

Technische Daten:

A318
Länge	31, 44 m
Spannweite	34, 09 m
Höhe	12, 51 m
MTOW	68 t
max. Nutzlast	15,1 t
max. Treibstoffkapazität	23 860 l
Max. Reichweite	5 950 km

A319
Länge	33, 84 m
Spannweite	34, 09 m
Höhe	11,76 m
MTOW	75, 5 t
max. Nutzlast	17, 9 t
max. Treibstoffkapazität	29 840 l
Max. Reichweite	6 850 km

DIE FLUGZEUGE

Der Airbus A319 geht mit Polarfuchs Misty in die Luft. 49 Flugzeuge dieses Typs sind für Frontier Airlines unterwegs.

An Airbus A319 taking off – this one with arctic fox Misty. There are 49 aircraft of this type operating on Frontier flights.

Seite 92/page 92:
Der Airbus A318 – hier mit Bartkauz Olli – ist das kleinste Mitglied der europäischen Flugzeug-Familie.
Foto: Manas Barooah

The Airbus A318 – like the one showing Great Grey Owl Ollie – is the smallest member of the Airbus family.
Photo: Manas Barooah

30. April 1996 den Liniendienst für Swissair auf. Die A319 ist knapp vier Meter kürzer als die A320. Sie befördert 124 bis 145 Passagiere. Die kleinere Schwester A318 lieferte Airbus am 21. Juli 2003 an Frontier aus – mit einem Grizzly auf dem Seitenleitwerk. Seinen Erstflug hatte der „Hundertsitzer" der Airbus-Familie am 15. Januar 2002 absolviert. 107 bis maximal 129 Passagiere kann der kleinste Airbus befördern.

Angetrieben wird die A319 von CFM56-5- oder von V2500A5-Triebwerken. Die A318 ist mit Motoren von Pratt&Whitney PW6000 oder CFM56-5B unterwegs. Die Reisegeschwindigkeit der A320-Familie liegt bei Mach 0,78.

Die Flugzeug-Familienmitglieder haben so viele Gemeinsamkeiten, dass sie wie ein einziger Flugzeugtyp betrieben werden können – mit identischem Cockpit, gleichen Flugeigenschaften, Systemen und Wartungsverfahren. Die Airlines wissen diese Kommunalität zu schätzen, denn bei einer gemixten Airbus-Flotte können die Piloten problemlos ohne viel Schulung von einem Cockpit ins andere umsteigen. Knapp 3 200 Flugzeuge der A320-Familie sind derzeit für knapp 200 Fluggesellschaften unterwegs (Stand August 2007), und das Auftragspolster umfasst rund 2 100 weitere Flugzeuge.

characteristics, on-board systems and maintenance routines. Airlines appreciate such commonalities. In a mixed Airbus fleet, these allow pilots to switch from cockpit to cockpit with little extra training. Just about 3,200 aircraft from the A320 family are operated by 200 airlines (as of August 2007). There are currently another 2,100 orders.

Specifications

A318

Overall length	103 ft 2 in
Height	41 ft 2 in
Wingspan	111 ft 10 in
MTOW	149,900 lb
Maximum payload	33,300 lb
Maximum fuel capacity	6,300 US gal
Range (max. passengers)	3,200 NM

A319

Overall length	111 ft
Height	38 ft 7 in
Wingspan	111 ft 10 in
MTOW	166,500 lb
Maximum payload	39,500 lb
Maximum fuel capacity	7,885 US gal
Range (max. passengers)	3,700 NM

Die Bilder *Pictures*

Seite 38/39
Denver International Airport – durch Frontiers Flotte wird er zum Tierpark.
Frontier's fleet turns Denver International Airport into a zoo.

Seite 40/41
Die Rotfuchs-Welpen „Mo" und „Jo" landen mit der A318 in Denver.
Red fox pups Mo and Jo arriving at Denver on their A318.

Seite 42/43
„Trixie", der Rotfuchswelpe, überholt mit der A319 in Denver United Airlines.
Red fox pup Trixie on their A319, passing a United Airlines aircraft in Denver.

Seite 44/45
Morgenstimmung in Denver mit „Fritz", der Schneeziege und „Foxy", dem Rotfuchs.
Denver: mountain goat Fritz and red fox Foxy at the break of dawn.

Seite 46/47
Das Leichtgewicht unter den Frontier-Tieren: „Hamilton", der Kolibri.
The leightweight in Frontier's zoo: Hamilton-the-Hummingbird.

Seite 48/49
Hier ist er zuhause: Maultierhirsch „Mel" posiert vor der Kulisse der Rocky Mountains.
In his habitat: mule deer Mel posing against the Rocky Mountain scenery.

Seite 50/51
Von rechts: „Sally", der Mustang, das Schwarzwedelwild „Domino" und Schwarzbär „Jo-Jo".
Left to right: black bear Jo-Jo, black-tailed deer Domino and Sally-the-Mustang.

Seite 52/53
Friedliche Begegnung am Airport: Kojote „Karl" trifft Gabelbock „Andy".
A peaceful encounter at the airport: Carl the Coyote meets Andy the Pronghorn.

Seite 54/55
Die vier Kaiserpinguine: Jim, Joe, Jay und Gary in Atlanta.
Jim, Joe, Jay and Gary - Emperor Penguins at Atlanta.

Seite 56/57
Kam soeben von Los Angeles nach Denver gehoppelt: das Waldkaninchen „Stu".
Just arrived at Denver from Los Angeles: eastern cottontail Stu.

Seite 58/59
Hat er sich etwa hier scheiden lassen? Jaguar „Sal" wird in Reno gesichtet.
Sal-the-Jaguar was sighted at Reno. Did he actually get a divorce?

Seite 60/61
Von links: Schwarzbär „Jo-Jo", Blaukopf-Sittich „Carmen", „Hank", der Rotluchs, Hermeline „Erma" und Gabelbock „Andy".
Left to right: black bear Jo-Jo, blue-crowned conure Carmen, bobcat Hank and ermine Erma.

DIE BILDER

Seite 62/63
Beim Start ist es schneller als das Taxi: „Cloe", das Rehkitz.
At take-off faster than a taxi: deer fawn Cloe.

Seite 64/65
Wem winkt sie hier in Denver wohl zu, die Trompeter-Schwanendame „Grace"?
Whom is Grace, the lady trumpeter swan, waving at in Denver?

Seite 66/67
Die Meeresschildkröte „Sheldon" gehört dem Frontier-Tierreich noch nicht lange an.
Sea turtle Sheldon is a greenhorn in Frontier's animal kingdom.

Seite 68/69
Von links die Stockente „O'Malley", der Elchbulle „Chocolate" und die Schnee-Eule „Doc".
Left to right: O'Malley-the-Mallard, Chocolate-the-Moose and snowy owl Doc.

Seite 70/71
Bison „Humphrey" ist mit dem kleinsten Airbus, der A318, unterwegs.
Humphrey-the-Bison travelling on the smallest Airbus type: the A318.

Seite 72/73
Sie fliegen mit der A319 auch südliche Ziele an: das Eisbär-Pärchen „Alberta + Clipper".
On their A319, polar bear couple Alberta and Clipper also fly to southern destinations.

Seite 74/75
Auf dem Flughafen Washington National: die Berglöwendame „Lola" mit Sohn „Max".
Mountain lioness Lola and her son Max at Washington National.

Seite 76/77
Durchsetzungsfähig und wehrhaft: „Stanley", das Dickhornschaf, unterwegs mit einer A319.
Assertive and resistant: bighorn sheep Stanley travelling on an A319.

Seite 78/79
Ein Walross ist zu schwer zum Fliegen? Beim Start in Atlanta beweist „Earl" das Gegenteil.
Who said a walrus was too heavy to fly? Earl proves them wrong at take-off in Atlanta.

Seite 80/81
„Jake" der Hirsch und Luchs-Kind „L.J." Die Abkürzung steht für „Larry junior".
White-tailed deer Jake and lynx kitten L.J. (Larry Jr.).

Seite 82/83
Gleich geht's los: „Rudy" der Waschbär, wird gleich in Denver zur Startposition rollen.
Ready for take-off: Rudy-the-Raccoon about to set off for the starting position.

Seite 84/85
Die Stacheln des Stachelschweins „Spike" haben keinen Einfluss auf die Aerodynamik.
Porcupine Spike's quills do not affect aerodynamics.

AUTHORS

Die Autoren *Authors*

Dietmar Plath

Der 1954 geborene Otterstedter gehört zu den erfahrensten Fotografen in der Welt zwischen Himmel und Erde. Über 110 Länder auf allen Kontinenten besuchte **Dietmar Plath**, um interessante Flugzeuge in den kühnsten und exotischsten Farben und Bemalungen oder vor faszinierenden Landschaften festzuhalten und der Öffentlichkeit zu vermitteln. Neben vielen Kalendern demonstrieren zahlreiche Luftfahrtbücher und Bildbände sowie eindrucksvolle Fotoreportagen in verschiedenen Fachmagazinen sein vielseitiges Repertoire. Seit 1997 ist er Chefredakteur von Aero International.
dietmar.plath@t-online.de

*Born in 1954 in Otterstedt (Northern Germany), Dietmar Plath is one of the world's most experienced photographers between heaven and earth. He has travelled to more than 110 countries on all the continents in order to capture and present to the public interesting aircraft in the most eye-catching and exotic colors and liveries and in fascinating landscapes. His varied repertoire is demonstrated not only by many calendars but also numerous aviation books and photo editions. Since 1997 he has been managing editor of Aero International.
dietmar.plath@t-online.de*

Sigrid Andersen

Tiere hat **Sigrid Andersen** schon immer geliebt. Die Liebe zu Flugzeugen kam erst im Alter von 40 Jahren. 1989 ging die gelernte Redakteurin bei Airbus in Deutschland an Bord, um in der Unternehmenskommunikation eine Kollegin im Erziehungsurlaub zu vertreten. Aus dem befristeten Einsatz wurde mehr, aus der Technik-Desinteressierten ein Luftfahrt-Fan. Bionik würde sie studieren, wenn sie noch einmal vor der Berufswahl stünde. Doch sind es nicht allein die technologischen Innovationen der fliegenden High-Tech-Produkte, die die 59-jährige Flensburgerin begeistern. Ihr haben es in erster Linie die Menschen angetan, die im Flugzeugbau arbeiten.

Sigrid Andersen has always had a soft spot for animals. Only at the age of 40 did she developed a liking for aircraft. In 1998, Andersen, a qualified editor, joined the German Airbus division to replace a colleague on long-term maternity leave. This temporary position was then extended. Andersen, then completely uninterested in technology, became a true aviation buff. If she again had to choose a career, she would do a course in bionics. 59-year-old Andersen from Flensburg in northern Germany is not only thrilled by flying high-tech products. She is particularly fond of all the people working in aircraft manufacturing.

Ein kostenloses Gesamtverzeichnis erhalten Sie beim
GeraMond Verlag
D-81664 München

www.geramond.de

Layout: imprint, Ilona Külen, Zusmarshausen
Übersetzung ins Englische/English translation: Andreas Greiser

Alle Fotos/photography: Dietmar Plath
außer Seite 92/except page 92 : Manas Barooah

Alle Angaben dieses Werkes wurden von den Autoren sorgfältig recherchiert und auf den aktuellen Stand gebracht sowie vom Verlag geprüft. Für die Richtigkeit der Angaben kann jedoch keine Haftung übernommen werden. Für Hinweise und Anregungen sind wir jederzeit dankbar. Richten Sie diese bitte an:

Otterstedter Verlag
Postfach 1135
D-28866 Otterstedt

Die Deutsche Nationalbibliothek – CIP Einheitsaufnahme
Ein Titeldatensatz für diese Publikation ist bei der Deutschen Nationalbibliothek erhältlich.

© 2008 by Otterstedter Verlag
© für diese Ausgabe GeraMond Verlag GmbH

Alle Rechte vorbehalten
Printed in Germany by Girzig&Gottschalk, Bremen
ISBN: 978-3-7654-7002-8